From Home
HOME *to*
HOME *to*

The Courageous Rescue of a
Hidden Child

Gloria Glantz

ISBN 978-1-64300-797-7 (Paperback)
ISBN 978-1-64300-798-4 (Hardcover)
ISBN 978-1-64300-799-1 (Digital)

Covenant Books, Inc.
11661 Hwy 707
Murrells Inlet, SC 29576
www.covenantbooks.com

DEDICATION

I wrote this book because of memories, buried and unburied, which have kept resurfacing in my life and because these testimonies need to be heard. This shameful, hateful period of humanity's history cannot be allowed to be forgotten, for it is a warning of our ability to invent unspeakable cruelty.

This book is written in memory of the one and a half million children whose lives were crushed, whose childhoods were stolen, whose potentials were never realized, and whose contributions will be missed eternally. In memory of my family, my parents, my brothers, my grandparents, who never got to know me and whom I outlived by the age of four. In memory of my people, the Jewish people, who died because they were born.

In memory of all those, of any race or religion, who died trying to stop the hate and the terror.

CABLE ADDRESS:
"JEWCON," MONTREAL

Canadian Jewish Congress

NATIONAL HEADQUARTERS:
1121 ST. CATHERINE STREET WEST,
MONTREAL—THIEPHONE PLATEAU 6891
Central Division Office: 150 Beverly Street, Toronto Western
Division Office: 402 Confederation Life Building, Winnipeg

NATIONAL OFFICERS	HONORARY VICE-PRESIDENTS	
SAMUEL BRONFMAN, PRESIDENT	REV. DR. H. ABRAMOWITZ	N. HEINISH
MICHAEL GARBER, K.C. VICE-CHAIRMAN, EXECUTIVE COMMITTEE	A. H. ARONOVITCH DR. D. M. BALTZAN	S. KRONICK J. I. OGLDAUM
MONROE ABBEY, VICE-PRESIDENT	S. DELKIN	S. PEARLMAN
SOL KAMEE, VICE-PRESIDENT	A. B. BENETT	LAZ. PHILIPS, K.C. O.B.E.
SEN. SADOWSKI, M.B.E. VICE-PRESIDENT	ALLAN BRONFMAN	B. ROBINSON. K.C.
JOSEPH H. FINE. HONORARY TREASURER	I. FREEMAN	F.I. SPIELMAN
H. M. CAIBERMAN, GENERAL SECRETARY	E.E. GELBER	CHAS, WALFISH
SAUL HAYES, EXECUTIVE DIRECTOR	M.A. GRAY, M.L.A	H. WOLOFSKY
		S.J. ZACKS

5

Mr. David Heiss,
Executive Director,   5th February, 1948.
2040, Blenry Street
Montreal

                                      Re: Deposit and/or Interested Party
                                      For child…PRZEPIORKA Gucia…

Please be advised that _____   Mr. Max Bernstein
                                _____ 1724 Popham Avenue
                                _____ Bronx. N.Y.
Has undertaken financial responsibility_____
has deposited here $_____
has undertaken to take the child in his home_____
Is a (n)_____uncle_____ (relationship).

Very truly yours,
M. SAALHEIMER

AFFIDAVIT

I, the undersigned, MAX BERNSTEIN, merchant, residing and domiciled at 1724 Popham Au, Bronx in the city of New York, in the State of New York, being duly sworn do depose and say:-

1. That I am an uncle of the orphan child GOCIA PRZEPIORKA, and am interested in rescuing her from Europe and bringing her to this continent;
2. That I have taken communication of both the affidavit and guarantee signed by Abraham Morantz, a friend of our family, and declare the statements therein to be true to the best of my knowledge and belief, and satisfactory to me and my wife as the only surviving blood relations of the said GOCIA PRZEPIORKA;
3. That I join in the guarantee of the said Abraham Morantz for the maintenance, upkeep, education and transportation costs of the said GOCIA PRZEPIORKA, guaranteeing the fulfillment of his obligation both to the Canadian Jewish Congress and to any other agency, governmental or institutional, which may have to expand money or services for the said child;
4. That as evidence of my financial ability to do everything I above assume, I annex hereto and make part hereof a true copy of my Federal Income Tax Return filed for the year;
5. That my financial status has not materially changed since the filing of such return, and it is a fair reflection of my present financial income.

AND I HAVE SIGNED,

Sworn to before me at Montreal
this 13th day of October, 1947

Commissioner of the Superior Court
District of Montreal

GUARANTEE

I, Abraham Morantz, of the city and District of Montreal, hereby undertake in connection with the entry of the child GOCIA PRZEPIORKA to the Dominion of Canada, to guarantee and do guarantee that the said child will be maintained and supported by me upon her arrival in Canada.

I further undertake to assume all the costs and expenses incurred for her transportation to Montreal, and for the maintenance of the child until her arrival in Montreal, the specific obligations assumed in the affidavit hereto attached to form part hereof.

I further declare that I will guarantee and indemnify the Canadian Jewish Congress for any obligation the Congress may incur as a result of its commitments in connection with the admission of the above described orphan child.

Witness: AND I HAVE SIGNED

AFFIDAVIT

I, the undersigned, ABRAHAM MORANTZ, butcher, residing and domiciled at 22 Fairmount Ave. W. in the City and District of Montreal, having been daily sworn do depose and say:-

1. That I am a citizen of Canada, and do make this affidavit in the support of the issuance of a visa or permit to GOCIA PRZEPIORKA for permanent entry into Canada under the terms and conditions enunciated by Order-In-Council P.C. 1647;

2. That the child is an orphan, bereaved of both parents, being a daughter of Esther Przepiorka and Mendl Przepiorka, both deceased;

3. That the child, born in Poland in 1939, is now being cared for in Sweden by the Association of Polish Jews in Sweden, and is living in a boarding house for children at Fiskeby-Norrköping, two miles outside of Stockholm Amk;

4. That I and my wife, who was a childhood friend of the late Esther Przepiorka, both of them hailing from the said district near Wangrow, Kel-Gredzie-Wojewodztwo-Warsawakie, Poland, are most anxious that the child GOCIA PRZEPIORKA, aged eight years, be permitted to enter Canada, so that we may maintain her and bring her up and look after her even as our own child;

5. That should she be granted such visa, I will be most willing to pay, and hereby undertake to pay for her transportation to Canada, and thereafter, to provide for her every need;

6. That I am willing and able to received, maintain and support the said GOCIA PRZEPIORKA, and hereby assume such obligations, guaranteeing that she will not at any time become a burden or public charge, and that she will be sent to day school at least until she is eighteen years of age, and will not be put to work unsuited for her years;

7. That the said GOCIA PRZEPIORKA is in good health and physical condition, and is normally sound to the best of my knowledge and belief;

8. That as evidence of my financial ability to do everything I above assume, I annex here to and make part hereof a true copy of Federal Income Tax return filed for the year 1945;

9. That my financial status has not materially changed since the filing of such return, and it is a fair reflection of my present financial income which has been derived from the same business for the last twenty-five years.

AND I HAVE SIGNED,

Sworn to before me at Montreal
this 13th day of October, 1947

Commissioner of the Superior Court
District of Montreal

PREFACE

This book was written not because I wanted to do it but because I needed to do it.

The process actually began in 1993, when I was diagnosed with breast cancer and on a chemotherapy regimen. I was told that about three weeks after starting chemotherapy, my hair would fall out. Heretofore, I always had many compliments about how thick, curly, and beautiful my hair was. I had a very expensive wig, also a cheaper one, and many snoods, kerchiefs, and head coverings. I was prepared, I thought.

Sitting on my couch one evening in November 1993, I put my hand through my hair. I had a whole handful of hair! I repeated that gesture again—and had another handful and another! My scalp was bare! Then it happened. I started to wail, scream, cry, sob, and pant. I was no longer in my commodious home on Long Island in 1993, but back in Wegrow, Poland, in 1942 with a man on a cross on the wall and a beautifully draped woman with a child on another wall. I was crying, screaming, and panting the same way as I had when my dark-haired, ashen-faced mother left me—forever. My gut hadn't forgotten. I was out of the Holocaust, but the Holocaust was not out of me.

In 2003 to 2004, I had the honor of participating in a writing workshop for survivors at the Holocaust Memorial and Tolerance Center in Glen Cove, New York. It was run by an organization called "Poets and Writers" and conducted by a published poet, Veronica Golos and her able assistant, Bonnie Marcus. It was financed through the generosity of the center's librarian, Marcia Posner; thus, at no charge to the participants. We were about eight survivors eager to put our thoughts on paper. We did various exercises to hone our craft and read aloud to the group. We got constructive criticism from our instructors and ideas to pursue various parts of our experiences.

Thus, I amassed a number of pieces I really liked and felt removed enough from the actual events as they occurred in the early part of my life. I was writing from a different perspective—the perspective of someone who had conquered my early fears and expectations; the perspective of a "successful" survivor with a family, home, career, friends and other fulfillments. I was encouraged to keep writing and use this material in a book.

Yet, somehow, I felt I was not able to write a full-length book about my experiences as a child because I had insufficient memories. I was told to write a children's book. I explored that idea as well, taking a one-day Gotham Writers workshop on children's writing in 2006 I wrote a page-numbered draft, and followed that up with a short workshop at the Port Washington Library run by Jane Breskin Zalben—an accomplished and well-known children's writer and illustrator. The idea of exploring my own childhood was tucked somewhere in my brain only to reappear in 2008, when I learned about another Gotham Writers workshop being given in New York City. It was a ten-week, thirty-hour course on Memoir and involved a commitment to go into a booth to have members of the class as well as the workshop presenter critique your work with written comments freely given on successes and redo of your pieces. One of the important nuggets of information I picked up there was that if I wasn't writing a biography, I really was able to write about the memories I did have as long as I was honest in depicting the character and the background atmosphere of the situation.

Fast forward to 2010, I was notified by the Hidden Child Foundation/ADL that Dr. Mordecai Paldiel, for twenty-four years in charge of the Righteous Among the Nations Department at Yad Vashem, was now in New York teaching at Stern College, and would be willing to help honor rescuers. I jumped at the opportunity and after three years of meetings and research, this honoring by Yad Vashem did take place in April of 2013. I had a big event in my town to honor that honoring (on November 24, 2013) with over five hundred people in attendance. I got many speaking engagements after that, and in the question periods, I was constantly asked, "Why don't you write a book?"

But still, I was too fearful, too busy, too overwhelmed, too unenthusiastic, too distracted to go any further. Sometime in the autumn of 2016, I pick up a book in the Port Washington library on the table of "good reads." *Big Magic*, by Elizabeth Gilbert. The subtitle on the cover says, "Creative Living beyond Fear." I am intrigued enough to start reading it. I could have used a bit of big magic at that time. I had the time, and the idea of writing was still embedded in me. I was ripe for writing now.

The years march on. Many memories of my youth are gone. Some memories I do have aren't even mine. They were contributed by various people who shared a specific time and place with me. My youth, too, is gone. So perspectives from this time and place inform much of the content. Last chance. It's time to unravel my past. But there is another important reason this book needs to be written. It has recently been noted that millennials have very little familiarity with, and knowledge of the Holocaust. Some have never even heard the word Auschwitz. The 1930s and 1940s are receding into forgetfulness. I feel this history must not be allowed to be forgotten. It should be taught, and its important lessons must be plucked from it. Unfortunately, we have not learned those lessons yet.

Elie Wiesel said: "In truth my major concern has always been the survivors . . . Did I strive to speak for them, in their name? I strove to make them speak." Thank you, Elie Wiesel. You have succeeded. I am speaking, retrieving my past.

Gloria Glantz

FOREWORD

by Dr. Mordecai Paldiel

Every survival story emanating from the Holocaust evokes a world of its own. None is similar to another, although they share some common traits, mostly of suffering and pain. But some also contain a few, but significantly important, sparks of light—the help received by strangers that made it possible for the narrators to survive. When speaking of Poland, it is well to remember that the German conquerors threatened the death penalty for anyone sheltering a Jewish person. There was also a lot of local antisemitism to go around. These factors combined to discourage many from extending a helping hand to Jews on the run, especially children. But there were exceptions. One was Maria Kowalczyk, who sheltered Gitl Przepiorka, today's Gloria Glantz.

Little Gitl was three years old when, on a cold dark night in 1942, she was turned over into the hands of Maria Kowalczyk by her mother, Esther Przepiorka, who had been residing in Węgrow. One can hardly grasp the traumatic experience of the little girl as she clutched her mother's coat and, screaming, asked not to be abandoned in the care of a stranger woman. She was never to see her mother again, nor her father Mendl. Both perished on different dates; the mother, in the gas chambers of Treblinka camp, as most of the other Jewish residents of Węgrow. In fact, little Gitl stayed under the loving care of Maria Kowalczyk (whom she adoringly referred to as "*Matka*") for some time after the war's end in May 1945, when she was taken away from Kowalczyk and placed in a children's home in Otwock, near Warsaw, and from there taken out of Poland to a children's orphanage in Sweden. There she stayed until her relatives in New York arranged for her to head to Montreal, Canada, into a welcoming Jewish family, although total strangers to Gloria, where she stayed for three years before finally being allowed to go to her relatives in New York, where she grew up, married, and raised a family of her own. The most harrowing years of her early childhood were, of course, the long years of the German occupation in Maria Kowalczyk's care, where extreme caution had to be taken for little Gitl, renamed Gucia Chanusha Kowalczyk, not to inadvertently disclose her Jewish origin. Mementos of these episodic encounters appear in this book.

I met Gloria Glantz (the former Gitl Przepiorka) in 2011, when learning of my association with the ADL/Hidden Children Foundation, she approached me to help her with submitting a request to Yad Vashem, in Jerusalem, to have the already departed Maria Kowalczyk awarded the title of "Righteous Among the Nations." I assisted her with writing her testimony, as well as collecting the testimonies of other Jews aided by this brave woman—Arnold Friedman, Morris Friedman, and Maryla Starr. In April 2013, Gloria Glantz was informed that her rescuer had indeed been added to the list of the Righteous Among the Nations as well as Maria's late husband, Michal. Both names now appear on the honor wall of the Yad Vashem Garden of the Righteous. This recognition was followed by a public ceremony on November 23, 2013, in Gloria's worshipping temple, The Community Synagogue, in Port Washington, Long Island.

This book retells Gloria's story in much greater detail.

What I find impressive in her story is not only the excruciating separation from her parents coupled with the years-long experiences of pains of fear, followed by more years of constant movement from one place to another, and into new strangers' hands. These experiences in themselves will rivet the reader's attention. Especially gripping and heartbreaking is the description of her forcible separation from *Matka* Kowalczyk at an airport in Poland when she rushed out of the plane about to take off to be again in the arms of her beloved *Matka* but sadly was never to see her again. Of greater significance, however, is that she emerged from that crucible to become a positive, forward-looking, and helpful person into a life upholding orientation. Gloria's story is proof that the fears by some Holocaust narrators that retelling the story of those years of darkness would fashion persons with a negative view of people and life with suspicion, distrust, and aggressiveness that such prognosis need not necessarily hold ground. This, at least, is not true in the case of Gloria Glantz and hopefully with many other survivors. As she beautifully stated in her testimony to Yad Vashem in response to a student's question of what she would say to her parents, were she given the chance, in an unreal situation, to see them again, she would have said, "You and your pain are not forgotten . . . The Jewish people still live . . . You have two beautiful grandchildren and now five great-grandchildren, who will pass on our heritage . . . You would have been proud of me, your youngest child. I have a rich and full life filled with love, friendship, family, and joy . . . My work enables me to make a difference in children's lives . . . My life is filled with music, a gift from you. You are alive in my heart always."

This is the kind of uplifting message that should help the reader, of whatever background, not to despair of life's sometimes bad and distressing experiences (commonly affecting most people at some point in their lives) but to hold their head up high and absorb the beauty that life has to offer, for there is a lot of goodness out there waiting to be grasped. One can find out more by reading Gloria Glantz's gripping story.

Mordecai Paldiel
Professor of Holocaust History, Stern College, Yeshiva University
Director of "The Righteous Among the Nations
Dept.," Yad Vashem, Jerusalem, 1982–2007

PART 1

&

POLAND

CHAPTER 1

A Walk in the Woods

Wegrow, 1942. My story starts with a walk in the dark woods in the summer of 1942. Estera Przepiorka, (PRZPIÓRKA) my mother, in a kerchief and ragged, loose dress holds me, her youngest child, Gitele, by the hand. In her left hand was a small cardboard suitcase and under her arm, close to her body, a down comforter, a *perineh*. There were fires in the woods and loud crashing noises like explosions.

"I'm cold," I whimpered.

We stopped intermittently, changing direction away from the fires. Then we continued quickly, with me trying to keep up with my mother.

"Walk quickly, *mine kind* (my child), as fast as you can."

I took a little hop and a run to keep up with my mother who was almost pulling my hand.

"Where are we going, Mama?"

She didn't answer, just breathed deeply and hurried on.

We reached a farmhouse. A large, broad-shouldered woman, a stranger to me, opened the door.

My mother put down the suitcase, looked at *Pania* (Mrs.) Kowalczyk. My mother knew her, I later learned, because her husband, Michal, was the custodian for the grounds of the leather factory my father and Uncle Moishe owned and operated. Then my mother looked at me, and in an iota above a whisper, uttered the life-altering words. "You have to stay here, Gitele."

We entered. I looked at the room; I looked at my mother. "And you, too, Mama?" She shook her head and began walking toward the door. "Wait!" I grabbed her coat and tried to clutch her knees. She left.

"I want my mama!" I screamed, then sobbed, and then panted. Who was this woman now talking to me? "Don't cry. You'll have a warm bath and a glass of milk. And tomorrow you'll be a big girl."

Finally and fitfully, I fell asleep. Upon awakening, I barely whispered, "Am I a big girl yet?" I had to become a big girl. That was the last time I saw my mother.

What had precipitated my mother's heroic and heartbreaking action? It must have been deep love and hope. She must have hoped that she could, at least, save her baby. As a mother now, I cannot imagine the courage she had to muster to leave her child with a relative stranger, with no assurance the child's life would be spared or that she would ever see her Gitele again.

CHAPTER 2

WEGROW. MY TOWN. CITATION #1

Jews had lived in Wegrow since the sixteenth century and were more than 50 percent of the total population when World War II broke out. The town was much older, though, founded in 1414. Jews settled there in sixteenth century under Lithuanian rule. Most retail business centered on the town square. Jews had to pay a special annual tax of two zlotys per household to live there. (*Beit Hatfutzot*, Israel, information flyer, 7/87).

In the second half of the eighteenth century, Wegrowers were cattle farmers, tailors, weavers, bakers, carters, and guild members. In 1794, a Hebrew printing press of *Nowy Dwor* printed books in Wegrow. In the 20th century, the knitting and tanning industry flourished. Wegrow, where Jews and Christians had lived in a love-hate relationship for over five hundred years, was one of the most ancient communities in Poland, with respected and honored rabbis, home of Chassidim, political parties, and ordinary hardworking people. There were a few merchants. Jack Kugelmass (#3) from a Ruined Garden Wegrow Jews cherished their religion. Itske Pilet, the *shamash*, would shout, "Into the shul!" before Shabbat. There was a large synagogue, the two-hundred-year-old *Beit Midrash*, and several smaller ones. #4 Jewish business men had to close their businesses before the Sabbath or be subject to economic boycotts and social ostracism. Citation #5 (Bielawski). Religious Jews had services in their homes, like my Grandfather Pinchas. *Shabbat,* the Sabbath, was a special time.

The town's people observed special Jewish traditions for weddings, childbirth, and other *simchas,* (happy events). When a bride and groom's family agreed to a match, there was a sealed document and a festive betrothal followed with feasting and even musicians. Ten days before the wedding, rich parents made a meal and invited the poor. The bride and groom fasted the day of the wedding. The bride sat on a podium and danced with the girls. Weddings sometimes lasted several days and consisted of many steps such as veiling the bride, her circling the groom three times, and recitation of the *sheva-brokhes,* (seven blessings for the bride and groom), a moment of privacy for the bride and groom, and lots of music. From a Ruined Garden pp.91-94.) #6 Kugelmass.

Wegrowers were kind and generous to the sick and the poor. These traits were evident when people faced serious illness, death of dear ones, or indigence. The psalm society recited psalms twice a day for seriously ill citizens. The burial society prepared the body of the dead, dressed it accordingly, and took the appropriate steps 'til burial. Prayer services were held for seven days.

There was even a special hostel for indigent people passing through on any day. On Shabbat, they were invited to dinner.

This small town had many activities: political parties, youth organizations to teach Yiddish, reading and writing, history, training for going to Palestine. There were even communist groups who met in the woods. There was also a movie house, a *kino* (cinema), where Jews and Poles sat together.

The Przepiorkas, my family, lived here.

https://kehilalinks.iewishgen.org/Wegrow/
vengrov-pre-war.html (Map) citation #7
http://kehilalinks.iewishgen.org/Wegrow/synagogue.html #8
Market square in Wegrow
http://kehilalinks.iewishgen.org/Wegrow/history.html Citation#9

Synagogue on the right (close-up)

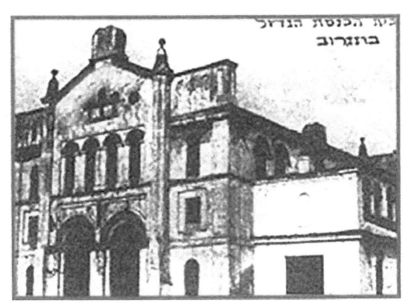

The great synagogue of Wegrow

CHAPTER 3

My Family

Esther Pniewska (or Finevasky var. of name), my mother, married Mendl Przepiorka, my father. As my aunt Norma, my father's youngest sister, related it, my mother was twenty-two and my father about thirty-two. On their wedding day, there was a terrible snow storm and many people could not make it to the wedding. My mother was known for her vocal ability. Even decades later, in 2011, this fact was recalled by Morris Friedman, a friend of my family and brother of Maryla Friedman who also was hidden by the Kowalczyks. Norma informed me my mother sang at her wedding in many languages—Yiddish, Polish, Russian, and possibly even German.

My mother's sister Chaiah married my father's brother, Moishe. They had four children, Esther, Fishl, Beile, Zelig and Itke. Esther was married and had a child. The entire family perished in Treblinka.

Their children (1) Itka and Bola Przepiorka (2) Fishel Przepiorka (Jordana's middle name is Chaiah).

https://kehilalinks.jewishgen.org/Wegrow/bola.html Citation 10

My father and Uncle Moishe operated a leather factory in the town square where they made the upper parts of boots and shoes, and we lived right in that complex, on Narutowicza 29. That street, according to Aunt Norma, was also called *Die Daitchishe Gas*, the German Street.

After I was born, we moved from there. About the same time, Norma elaborated, my father actually bought the building where his factory was located. Many years later, in 1957, in America, there was an opportunity to get compensation for property taken by the Germans during WWII. My Aunt Esther and Uncle Max engaged a lawyer, and I received $3,000 for my father's factory.

These two brothers, my father and Moishe, employed Michal Kowalczyk as their handyman and caretaker, with whom they had a good relationship. My father had lent him money, and they were in good terms. My father's charisma and good business acumen led many Polish teenagers to seek apprenticeships in his shop. He travelled to Warsaw (about fifty miles away) frequently on business. Still, he had a reputation in the family of being a bit rebellious. He smoked in secret—on the Sabbath, *Shabbat!* (forbidden by strict Jewish law). Because of his long work days, travel, and my toddler years, I didn't get to know him very well. But when he tickled me, I would probably have been able to smell the leather on his hands. Morris Friedman told me that my father was always joking and telling amusing stories. I mentioned this to our son, Craig, who welled up with tears. He possesses this similar charismatic trait of his grandfather, whom he would never know.

My father's family included my grandfather Pinchas and grandmother Rachel, and their ten children. From oldest to youngest, they were: Shlomo, Moishe, Yosef, Mendl, Esther, Pearl, Sarah, Fishl, Avraham, and Norma. Aunt Norma helped Grandma Rachel cut patterns and sew custom-fit clothes. That is how Grandma Rachel supported this large family, as Grandpa Pinchas studied the Torah most of the time, especially in his older age. They lived in Rozbitche, about 12 km, (2 and ½ mi.) walk from Wegrow, where he had previously owned a store later operated by my uncle, Yosef. Yosef and his wife Malka had three children, namely Chaitshe, Yankele, and Rivkele. Every Rosh Hashanah and Yom Kippur there was a *minyan* in Grandma and Grandpa's house in Rozbitche for about thirty to forty people. That house was for praying.

Uncle Moishe and my father were officials in the town. They were spokesmen for the Jewish community and were more assimilated than some of their siblings. They were fluent in Polish and highly respected by other Jews in the town. Uncle Shlomo, on the other hand, had a beard, dressed in the traditional religious garb (long black coat and hat), and was considered one of the *Aleksander Chasidim,* one of the *Talmidei Chachamim*, (wise and learned men). He was the one to turn to for answers to any Judaica question. He is also reputed to have had a beautiful voice, chanting on Shabbat and holidays, sending prayers to God.

<<Note: See #11 at the end of part 1: The Alekxander Chasidic movement flourished in Poland from 1880 until it was decimated by Nazi Germany during World War II. Now nearly extinct, the Aleksander Hasidim were one of the largest Hasidic groups in pre-Holocaust Poland. Today, Aleksander Chasidim can be found in communities in Israel, the United States, Switzerland, Antwerp, London, and Australia. https://www.geni.com/proiects/Alexander-Rabbinical-Dynasty/68 source # 11>>

My Mama, Estera Pniewska Przepiorka, was a teacher. She had deep set, inky eyes and a dark mole above her lip. She wore her black hair straight back in a bun. Her beautiful voice, and one of her songs, even today, reverberate in my conscience at night, and I sing it silently to myself. Some of the words were: *Shlof, shlof, shlof. Der tateh vet kumen fun dorf, vet er brengen an eppeleh, vet zein gezunt in kepeleh . . . vet er brengen a neeseleh, vet zein gezunt in feeseleh* (Sleep, sleep, sleep, your daddy will come home from town, he will bring an apple, so your head will be healthy…he will bring a nut, and your feet will be healthy). This song still haunts me, lovingly.

Her family came from another town, Pultusk, so I didn't get to know them as well as my father's family. She was the oldest of six siblings: Chiah, Blumcheh, Frimet, Edith, Esther, and a brother, Meier. My father and his nine siblings lived close by and there were many in-law aunts and uncles and their families, and a slew of boy and girl cousins.

Our immediate family was much more assimilated than other Jews in town. My father was clean-shaven, and wore beautiful clothes, not the long black coat and hat of the religious Jews. While he respected his father and spoke to him in Yiddish, in our home we all spoke Polish. My brothers took all their subjects in Polish public school, not a Cheder, a Jewish school. According to one of the young Wegrow residents, a boy whose last name was Ptak and whose descendants survived and lived in my uncle's building, they were even introduced to silent movies. Once a week, they could see Charlie Chaplin and buster Keaton. But Jewish students at these public schools were subjected to all forms of bullying by teachers and other students, including having stones thrown at them as they walked to and from school. I surmise that my brothers were subjected to the same mistreatment. (https://kehilalinks.iewishgen.org/Wegrow/ptak-4.html) Citation #12

This was a *Shabbat* at my house—a white cloth, wine at the table, my father in a tie, and my mother, who was pregnant and in her eighth month with me is also in fine clothes. My brothers are well dressed. There are flowers on the table.

I was with my family for only my first three years and have few memories. I do remember playing hide-and-seek with my two brothers, Zelig and Yitzchak, and hiding under the bed. I remember my mother singing lullabies to me every night to put me to sleep. "Please don't stop, Mama. Keep singing," I pleaded, begging her to continue. I wanted to hear her voice as I fell asleep. The tradition continued. My five grandchildren, as toddlers, were serenaded by me at bedtime. They loved the Yiddish songs I sang. Lexi, my youngest granddaughter, would ask, "What does that mean, Grandma?" Even my adopted nephew, Robert (now around sixty), remembers me at age twenty-four singing to him before bedtime when he was four.

Our family had the luxury of going to the country, a small farm village called Jarnic, in the summer with other aunts, uncles, and cousins. But I don't remember if my father's comfortable living allowed us to have running water and indoor plumbing or necessitated the use of an outhouse. And being with my father until I was only two, I was probably not even toilet-trained and still in cloth diapers.

When the Germans arrived, I was just a few months old. Zelig and Yitzchak were already about nine and twelve. Zelig was dark and handsome, with big brown eyes, and excelled in the "Gymnasium" school in a broad range of educational subjects taught in Polish. Polish schools started around age four. Yitzchak, my younger brother, suffered from *strabismus* (crossed eyes). I only have one very clear picture of him, and he is squinting. I, too, was born with crossed eyes. Aunt Norma told me I had a very long and difficult birth but a joy-filled arrival. Regina Akerman, another Wegrow resident, whose mother was my mother's best friend, recalled her visit to our home when I was born. It was as though a little princess had arrived! On a more recent afternoon, (she was now Regina Friedman), a Sunday in November of 2011, she also related how my father had pleaded with Michal and his wife Marianna to shelter his baby daughter. As it turned out, he was murdered before knowing that his wish had been granted.

I celebrate my birthday on May 22. It is an approximate date, as no papers are extant having been destroyed in Wegrow during the war. According to my Aunt Norma, it was after Pesach, in spring. It is very cold in Poland so it didn't feel like spring until May. When I came to America, we picked May 22, an approximate date, but the year 1939 is exact. Although it was an inauspicious time for a Jewish child to be born in Poland, I had a good, normal life with much family—cousins, aunts and uncles, grandparents all close for this little Gitele Przepiorka. Przepiorka means a little bird, an apt name for me at that time. I was free, and there was singing. Then this little bird had to leave her safe, warm nest and fly away, again and again and again.

CHAPTER 4

UNWELCOME INTRUDERS, THE NAZIS ARRIVE

Wegrow and Warsaw were overtaken by the German army just twenty days apart, Wegrow, some fifty-five miles from Warsaw on September 7, 1939, (according to *Last Jew from Wegrow*—Bielowski citation #13) and Warsaw on September 27, 1939. The two cities could not have been more different, the former a large metropolitan area with a Jewish population of 393,950 in 1939, and the latter, a *shtetl*, with only about six thousand Jews. The town was six miles wide. There were only two cars. Horse-drawn carriages made up the traffic.

Malka Weisblatt, in *Sefer Zikaron*, describes the vicious invasion of the Nazis as "hell in the world" (citation 14). She wasn't allowed to give out food to the unfortunates in Wegrow. Some had gathered straw to sleep on, and Germans poured water on them to add to the discomfort. They took her brother to the town square and made him dance and forced people to hit each other.

On *Yom Kippur* (The Day of Atonement), September 23, 1939, they took the chief rabbi, Jacob Mendl Morgenstern, to the market place, made him sweep it from end to end, and put the refuse and horse manure in his velvet hat to bring it to the dump. When he completed this chore, the next order was "Undress!" As he removed his *tallit* (prayer shawl), a soldier bayoneted him. He was the last rabbi of Wegrow.

The same month and year, September 1939, my father was arrested by the Polish Blue Police, possibly because he was considered wealthy, and also an alderman in the Jewish community. He was released back into the Wegrow ghetto, as his death certificate indicates.

When Wegrow became a ghetto in 1940, it was not walled or enclosed like some of the larger ghettos, but many Jews from neighboring towns such as Pultutsk, Kaluszyn, Tishnitz, Wyszkow, and Pabiance were forced into it. The Germans picked a *Judenrat (a Jewish leadership position)* to administer the ghetto and pass their edicts through him. The Jewish population in Wegrow grew tremendously from about 6,000 to possibly 11,000 according to Professor Jan Grabowski, who is doing research on wartime Wegrow. The predominant conditions of the ghetto were hunger, disease, and death.

The day after *Yom Kippur*, September 1942, Shraga Feivel Bielawski's neighbor, Shlomo Przepiorka, my father's oldest brother, told him that "Wegrow is surrounded by SS troops." When the Germans entered, there were decrees immediately. (The Last Jew from Wegrow, Shraga Feivel Bielawski, edited by Louis W. Liebovich, p.57.) Citation #15

Every Jew had to step off the sidewalk when he saw a German soldier.

All Jews over twelve must wear a white, four-inch band with a six-pointed blue star on it on their right arm. My brother, Zelig, had to wear one.

All synagogues were now closed.

No Jew could buy food in a grocery, only rations. The weekly ration for a family of four is one pound of meat, one-half pound of sugar, and one-half pound of butter.

All Jews had to observe a five-o'clock curfew. Jews could not leave their houses or be in the streets after five o'clock.

In addition, by 1941, if a Pole wanted a Jewish business, he would simply tell the housing authority established in 1939, and they would evict the Jewish owner. Thus, my father was probably no longer running his factory and making a living. The soldiers needed those nice leather boots, but my father was training Poles to run the business. In addition, Jews were no longer allowed to own property, so that building, too, was appropriated by the Germans. My cousin Sam, (who became my adopted brother in 1952), once said that if a Polish kid wanted your bicycle, you had better give it to him. That was the norm.

Our family was in economically dire straits. If I were older than three, perhaps I could have summarized the events in this manner:

Thursday	July 23, 1942	7,300	Warsaw	13,800	Leon Filkelstein survivor	Treblinka becomes fully operational.

The world is torn—we wake to the startling news.
People are tortured, halved, and quartered,
Families are shredded and voices are stilled.
He who lies down at night moans, or may not wake,
As the moments slip away
Repair the broken world, we long for it.

One is startled, knowing that all that has been planted.
Has not, nor will ever bloom,
But always we strive upward and hope.

Treblinka was one of the six killing camps built specifically for Jews, though others died there. Wegrow, my town, is listed in the chart below.
https://en.wikipedia.org/wiki/Timeline_of_Treblinka_extermination_camp Cit. 16
There were eight columns in the timeline with the following information.

Thursday	July 23, 1942	7,300	Warsaw	13,800	Leon Filkelstein survivor	Treblinka becomes fully operational.

Day #	Day of Week	Date [1]	Number of Deportees	Deported from	Cumulative total deportees	Known deportees	Major Events

Sent to Treblinka 8.300 deportees 411.741 =cumulative total deportees

Tuesday	September 22, 1942	8,300	Węgrów	411,741

283	Friday	May 1, 1943	Węgrów	Berek Lajcher, Treblinka revolt leader	Final Węgrów Ghetto liquidation

About one hundred Jews remained to clean up the mess from the first deportation and were sent to Treblinka in the second deportation in May 1, 1943. Among these innocent victims were my mother and brothers. When I was with *Matka*, and Arnold Friedman came to visit his sister and mother also hidden by my rescuer, Maria Kowalczyk, I remember Maria saying to him, "Are they gone yet?" and he answered, "Yes."

Even now over seventy years after the war, I marvel at the meticulousness of record keeping, like the days of the week the events occurred, and an exact, unrounded number of victims.

377	Monday	August 2, 1943	Treblinka revolt erupts. Some 300 prisoners performing forced labor, aware that the SS will soon kill them, stage an uprising after the initial date of the revolt set for June 15 was postponed due to grenade detonation at the undressing area. Prisoners quietly seize weapons from the camp armory, set fire to barracks, and storm the main gate. Hundreds attempt to climb the barbed-wire fence, but the SS with *Trawniki guards* kill two-thirds of them with machine-gun fire. Less than a hundred escaped successfully, chased in cars and on horses. Camp deportations and gassing operations halt the following month. [10]

William Schneiderman, back row, standing with a group of Treblinka escapees, first on right (Picture contributed by the Schneiderman family)

Aunt Norma's second husband, William Schneiderman, then called Wolf Schneidmann, (Uncle Willie to me) participated in the uprising. He succeeded in escaping, but tragically, as he had already lost his wife and five sons there. He matter-of-factly recounted his hours as a roofer. While repairing the roof of the area that housed the staff, he would see trains filled with people arriving continuously, but the camp population never increased.

The ghetto was liquidated and the first deportation to Treblinka, about twelve miles away, occurred on Yom Kippur, September 22, 1942. Hans Frank, the German governor general of Poland, appeared explaining that three hundred were needed for labor, nothing would happen to them. They pulled people out of hiding places such as chimneys and cellars and marched them to the cemetery where a ditch had been prepared and shot them. The Jewish police dug holes and buried them all night. They shot Jews as they were being hurried to the town square where there were wagons for the old and ill, and the men, (unlike most others who went there by train) walked to Treblinka. Several thousand Jews from the Wegrow ghetto were forced to walk about twelve to fourteen miles, to this concentration camp. According to Bielawski, *Last Jew of Wegrow,"* the Nazis shot one thousand Jews during the liquidation. Obviously, my father was not among them as he was killed before the camp began its killing spree. A question still pierces me about the circumstances of the deaths of my dear family members. My thoughts about their last suffering moments do not diminish with the flow of time. Cit. #17

PRZEPIURKA Mendl   650 111
od. PRZEPIORKA
Pinchas & Rachel Rubinson   jüd.
Grow   poln.
9.39 verhaft., Wengrow
7.40 Gh. Wengraw
Anf. 41 umgekommén
L. Adr. Wengrow, Narutowicza 29

BA f. Wg. Trier

f. RA Kohn, Mil.   N.

#18 International Red Cross document =
my father's death certificate

CHAPTER 5

LOOKING BACK

Securing my father's death certificate (above) put some of my history in perspective. The date of his death indicates he died or perished at the beginning of 1941, a date corresponding to the eviction of Jewish business owners. I can just imagine the scene of a leather booted German soldier entering his shop and demanding the keys and money of the factory, and my father shaking his head, or maybe opening his mouth to protest, and being shot on the spot. *Verhaft* means arrested, detained. My father was arrested in September 1939 as soon as Germans entered Poland. *Umgekommén* means perished, or died. He was about forty-seven or forty-eight when he perished (read murdered). Every picture I have of him is a professional one, a well-dressed, handsome man. If only I could say a few words to him, these are possibly what I might say:

My Father's Shoes

The leather is supple, yet sturdy; the stitching perfectly aligned, your fingers having deftly measured each stitch in its correct and precise position. The leather smells like real leather. Your hands smell the same. Your shoes are city shoes. You were always so well-dressed. In each picture you look elegant—a tie, or just an open collar over jacket lapels for less formal occasions. Did you wear those shoes at town meetings? On Rosh Hashanah? At weddings or B'nai Mitzvah? Or maybe brises. There were so many children in our family.

You must have made Zelig's and Yitzchak's first shoes. And later, their boots for the winter. And maybe you even made my first shoes. You were no longer around for the bigger sizes. You died without the knowledge that your pleas to the Kowalczyks had been heeded and your Gitele was indeed being sheltered, protected, and loved by them. And she has lived to become a grandmother.

You were an expert with leather. Many young boys in town sought to be apprenticed to you.

But your shoes defined you. From the bottom up, you were a gentleman. And from the top down, you were a man. My dear, father. I hardly knew you.

Or I can write a message to my father in poetic form:

Perhaps
(composed Dec. 14, 2017)

Perhaps you read to me,
Or tickled me to make me laugh,
Or hugged me in the morning
Before your hands were leather-smelling too,
Perhaps you kissed me late at night
When I was deep in dreaming,
Perhaps, Daddy, I hardly knew you.

In pictures you are debonair,
Dark, well-dressed, distinguished.
I learned you were in politics
In the shtetl that we lived in;
I heard you were a rebel,
Smoked in secret on Shabbat
Rode to sin-filled, Warsaw, too
Alas, I hardly knew you.
You might have helped me ride a bike
Let go when I was able,
Or maybe you'd have blessed me
At a Shabbat dinner table.
Or maybe you'd have had such pride in me
As I danced and sang with mama.
You might have clapped, or mama too
Alas, I hardly knew you.
I now have dark and curly hair
Perhaps some more traits of you,
But the memory so dim, unclear
The loss so daunting, deep,
"Daddy's little girl" you'd put to sleep,
Alas, I hardly knew you.

Misery was omnipresent. All families that had more than a kitchen and one bedroom had to give the other rooms to other Jews. From the above document, it seems our home had to give up its other rooms to other families, as our address is listed, Narutowicza 29. And every Jew living in a house or apartment, even if they owned it, had to pay monthly rent to the Rent Bureau, or be evicted. Men were sent out on work detail and came back beaten, starved, and exhausted. Was my father one of them? Was my older brother, Zelig?

My mother, under forty years of age, and alone, responded to these frightening and escalating events as well as to the rumors of killing and torture passed on by two escapees from the Treblinka death camp, heroically and selflessly. She wanted to save me, her baby, to spare me the horrors that surely awaited.

Since that life-changing, life-saving event, I have given great thought throughout my life, to what I wish I could say to my parents and other members of my family if I could speak to them. These are the letters I composed:

Dear Mama and Papa,

I wish I could speak with you again. The first time I told some of my sixth graders that you left me with a stranger, they were shocked. "How could a mother do that?" "That was terrible!" They didn't get it.

I remember our parting well. The muscles in my body remember it well, and my gut will never forget it. My chest was constricted as if by a tight rope. Breathing was gasping and labored. The wailing was fueled by all the vital capacity of my three-year-old lungs. I was terrified! I didn't know Pania Kowalczyk. I'm sure you prepared me for my first and only meeting with her. But when you closed the door behind you, my world collapsed.

You judged her well. Though no one could take your place, she made a valiant effort to make me feel loved. I remember the terror and the numbing sadness of the ensuing weeks and months. I ate little, cried often, and smiled rarely. I aged rapidly, and morphed into a quiet, serious older kid with a new identity, and new religious symbols.

Even my new name has become a source of confusion. Maria Kowalczyk called me Gucia, and that's the name I remember having 'til the age of eight, but I was told, in 2011, by Arnold Friedman, whose sister was also hidden by Maria and Michal Kowalczyk, that I was called Chanusha! (On new documents, I have several other names in addition to those). So much confusion for me, Mama. No games of hide and seek with Yitzchak and Zelig, or with any other children. It was a new type of hiding—to stay alive.

But I don't remember being angry with you. Perhaps I have relegated the anger to the inner recesses of my soul, because I now know why you left me. I, too, am now a mother. This decision you made must have been even more difficult for you. At age three, one has more resilience than at thirty-three. Psychologists hold that the first three years of a child's upbringing are of supreme importance in that child's growth and future capacity to handle the vicissitudes of life. I know my first (and only) three years with you were filled with love, sweetness, family, and security. Without knowing the horrors of the future, you fortified me for what was to come. Your decision probably filled you with dread, doubt, and guilt; but it was fueled by hope and love. Staying with you, your little Gitele would surely die. Perhaps she would live away from you. You gave me life twice.

To me, you are a hero! What pain you must have endured even before the indescribable agony of going to your death with your sons, your brothers, sisters, nieces, and nephews in Treblinka. Somewhere in the crevices of your tormented heart, perhaps you had the hope that your youngest, your baby, would live.

Our family was steeped in the teachings of Torah, especially by Grandpa Pinchas, who studied all day, and Uncle Shlomo, who was one of the Talmidei Chachamim. How I wish they could know that the pain and torture of the Jewish people is not forgotten. The Jewish people are still here. I wish I could have gotten to know our family a bit better. That I could have heard some of grandpa's wisdom, and I could have told him that as of May 14, 1948, we now have our own land, Eretz Yisrael. I wish I could have heard Uncle Shlomo's sweet voice singing the comforting *nigunim* (repetitive tunes) that enhanced the liturgy.

You have two humane, intelligent, and delightful grandchildren. You would have loved them as much as they missed not having you as grandparents. Your grandson, Craig, has your deep-set eyes, Mama, and the handsome face of his Uncle Zelig. He is charismatic, intelligent, and has a great sense of humor. Your granddaughter is astute in the business world, as you were, Papa. She is a wonderful mother, always going all out for the benefit of her children. She is sharp, well-liked, and lovely to look at.

You would recognize me even today. The birthmark you had, Mama, above your lip, I have on the right side of my face. I still have that curly hair, though it is more gray than black. You would have been proud of me, your little princess baby. I have a rich life, filled with love, friendship, family, and joy. I have been blessed with good health for most of my life and have been privileged with educational opportunities. My life's work has enabled me to touch the lives of children, and teach them the lessons of humanity and tolerance, so that there will never again be another Shoah against any group of people.

In addition, mother, I sing in a choir, attend concerts, and listen to opera. I can sing many Yiddish songs to my own grandchildren, some of which you sang to me. My life is filled with music, your precious gift to me. The memory of you is a blessing.

With love and remembrance,
Your Gitele

My grandfather had a different fate from the rest of my family. He did not experience the horrors of the camp but lived his last days as a victim of the brutality of Polish thugs who beat him so violently that he succumbed a week later.

Where Is Your Grave, Grandpa?

The thick memorial candle flickers in the darkness. The burial is over. In your simple white linen slip, you were buried, Pinchas Przepiorka, son of Itche Faivl. It is no wonder the wheel of the carriage bringing your plain pine box to the cemetery got stuck at the Iron Gate. It was no longer possible for a Jew to possess anything in good condition. All that could be heard was the sound of sobs of your remaining children.

No flag adorns your grave, no flower, no stones from visitors who could not pierce the barbed wire to place the little witnesses of memory.

But from cradle to grave you were a dedicated son of Israel, defender of God's book, a perpetual provider of wisdom, too soon, too brutally brought to your resting place. No lack of stones or visits can deny that truth.

Where is your grave, Grandpa Pinchas? My grandfather with the piercing green eyes, and a flowing beard of gray. Ten children you fathered. Some were God-fearing, some rebellious, all respectful of your knowledge, and your quiet wisdom. The lights of Shabbat candles weekly glowed as brightly as your eyes. The *zmirot* of your sweet-voiced first born, Shlomo, could be heard in the *shtiebl* (a prayer room in a home).

Your goal, son of Israel, was to nourish your Jewish soul. With each passing *parsha* (section of the Torah) each week, you loved and lived the book, the Torah scroll. You chanted, prayed, discussed, learned, and taught.

But you were the Jew, the Christ killer, the cause of all problems, political and economic. You stuck in their craw. They pulled your beard. Each hair a symbol of your devotion to your faith. Each painful pull a dedication to your God, the God of Abraham, Isaac, and Jacob. The God of Pinchas, Esther, Mendal, Fishl, Yosef, and Shlomo. The God of Sarah and Esther. The God of your noble wife, Rachel, the caring mother of your children, shot by a Polish policeman in 1942. (Cit. 19) At least you were no longer alive to know of her bitter end.

Your prayers did not reach. Your wisdom was not prized, your Jewish life not valued. They drained your strength, your blood they spilled. You could no longer live this way. At least you had a funeral. But where *is* your grave, Grandpa Pinchas?

I once stood upon a gravestone in a tiny cemetery in 1993. It was unmarked, ungroomed, broken, bare. Perhaps it was yours, Grandpa. Perhaps it remains. You were the only one with a funeral. We *could* grieve for you. You were our symbol of faith, of heart, of knowledge, of dedication, and religious fervor. But there are no stones placed *lovingly* on your tombstone. Your children, your grand-children, your friends, could never go to visit you, to remember you, talk of you, cherish their memories of you. The barbed wire forbade them to give you the respect you deserved. They are no more, and so unkindly cut down, some in their vibrant youth, and some in wise age. Gladly would you have gone in their stead al Kiddush Hashem, for the sanctification of God's name.

But at least, you once did have a funeral and a grave, Grandpa.

CHAPTER 6

A Different Nest: Living,
Loving, Leaving

As a three-year-old, I did not appreciate or understand what my mama had done and felt tortured in my own way. I was now known as Gucia Kowalczyk, with a new identity and new religious traditions. My identity now had to be congruent with my ability to pray to Jesus and Mary. There was a picture of the *Matka Boska* (Blessed Mother Mary) above my bed, and a picture of her son, Jesus, hanging on the opposite wall, his long hair crowning his gentle face. The cross bearing him was in the kitchen area.

Where were Zelig and Yitzchak? My mama? I was too young to understand why this was happening. I knew something was greatly amiss, but I was too traumatized to ask questions. I became a quiet and serious child. *Matka*, with her wide shoulders and long arms, warmed me with her hugs. She put her fingers through my frizzy hair and put a bow in it, especially when we went to church each Sunday. She made sure I had a clean body, heating the little wooden tub of my bath water on the stove, and preparing clean clothes. She tried to keep me sated, and even let me milk the cow with her so I could understand why there was a huge vat of fresh milk in the kitchen.

One day I asked for a glass of milk with my *kielbasa* (salami) sandwich. She said: "You can't have milk with *kielbasa*. You're Jewish." She immediately put her finger to her mouth. "But don't tell anyone." Years and years later, I am still trying to understand this—was she trying to keep some of my heritage alive in me? Was she trying to help me understand that being "Gitele" was dangerous? (Milk and meat cannot be eaten in the same meal according to strict Jewish Law.)

One day, I innocently entered the barn. There I saw two legs sticking out in the hay! I ran into the house screaming wildly, "There are Jews in the barn! There are Jews in the barn!" I had no idea what the word "Jews" meant. I must have heard the word used in a way that made me feel afraid.

"Don't worry, I took care of it," *Matka* said. It wasn't until years after I left Poland that I came to understand what she meant. There *had* been two Jewish women in the barn, thirteen-year old Maryla Friedman, and her mother Malka, whom Pania Kowalczyk was also hiding. But because Michal, her husband, drank heavily, *Matka* was concerned that if he got drunk, he might reveal that they were hiding Jews. So she transferred them to her attic space.

I once saw Michal hold a knife to *Matka*'s throat. Did he know they were in the barn and want her to force the Friedmans out? Surely, he must have known of the edict that anyone helping a Jew would be killed. I was terrified and stood frozen. That scene stayed with me for many years and contributed to my fearful behavior near men even when I was in a safe space. I actually discussed this issue in 2015 with Maryla Friedman, now Marilyn Starr. She said Michal was very fearful of keeping them. But they actually gave him an alternative scenario that would have been worse. They said: "If you let us go, we have no safe place to go. The chances are good that we will be caught. And they will torture us into telling them who kept us until now. And we will probably not be strong enough to withstand that torture and give your name. Then they will certainly come back and kill you."

Once again, *Matka*'s quick thinking led to her moving the Friedmans from the barn to the attic. By doing this secretly, she made Michal believe that she *had* made them leave. Indeed, as confirmed by Regina Akerman in her 2012 testimony, Michal did *not* know they were in the attic.

More than fifty years later, Maryla confided that she could peek out of the attic and envy this *przepiorka* (little bird) free to eat cherries and dance in the sunshine. Thanks largely to Maria's humanity, they also survived the war. Yes, her humanity gave this little *przepiorka* a more normal life. What a chance she took by having me out in the open, playing in the sunshine, not hidden and unable to move in a tight cellar or attic space! What trust she had in me, that I would measure up to the demands of having a new identity, that I would do as I was told, and l would not betray her and her family by slipping into a Jewish mode.

In the winter, when snow was knee-deep, there was the beautifully decorated Christmas tree in the room where I slept. The colorful round glass ornaments hung among the green sprinkled bell and star-shaped cookies. If I felt like having a snack in the middle of the night, I could help myself to one of those ornaments. The first three years of my time with my family gradually dissolved like sugar in hot water.

But my new life wasn't sweeter. No more *Shabbat*. No more *Chanukah*. My Sunday visits to the church in the town square were obligatory and silent. "Do as I do, don't ask questions" was the message I got. Yet the repetition of these rituals over time helped me to become comfortable with these new traditions and common prayers. Still, where were all the cousins, the children? No hide and seek games, no toys. I was now alone with *Matka* most of the time. There was a *matka*, but there wasn't a *tata* (father). I did not see Michal Kowalczyk very often. He didn't interact with me. He didn't tickle me. I missed the father I barely knew.

But their adopted daughter, Stanislava, about nineteen or twenty years old, who was called Stanka, spent time with me when she could, always treated me with gentleness and spoke to me softly. According to Arnold Friedman, the brother of Maryla Friedman, *Matka* once showed him a cake when he visited to see his sister and mother at Christmas and told him to have some. She said he reminded her of a boy she once had, and had died, and she added, "If Jozef survives, then we will all survive." (Arnold had false papers and used the name Jozef Kierszykowski) When he came to visit his sister and mother, he saw me at about three years of age. (The only man who I remember bouncing me on his knee was Arnold Friedman, who died on Rosh Hashanah of 2017 at age ninety-six).

Even though *Matka* protected me fiercely, the overall anti-Semitic environment, often expressed in German, impacted me negatively into adulthood. I heard an expression, *ferfluchte Jude*, damned Jew. Even when I was twenty-four, safely in America, I nearly flew out of my seat when going on a summer vacation trip with my friend Carole to Vienna on a train, an immigration official in uniform turned on the car lights and announced in a loud voice, *"Pass control!"* Subsequently, in the Vienna hotel, there was an elevator with a glass front door. We always felt as though we were being watched as we went up to our room. Not only that, the employee at the registration desk demanded our passports for the duration of our stay there. Our names were Gloria Bernstein and Carole Taback.

Even a kind act by a German such as a woman offering to share her cookies with us on the train made me feel ill at ease.

Danger was ever-present. And even at such a young age, I understood I had to hide my identity as a Jew. And there was a very good reason Poles were hesitant to help Jews even if they were so inclined. Rescuers had many reasons to be fearful of their neighbors. The laws that were promulgated by the Germans flamed this fear.

The Sheltering of Escaping Jews
(original German at the end of Part I)

There is a need for a reminder, that in accordance with paragraph 3 of the decree of October 15, 1941, on the Limitation of Residence in General Government (page 595 of the GG Register)

Jews leaving the Jewish Quarter without permission will incur the death penalty.

According to this decree, those knowingly helping these Jews by providing shelter, supplying food, or selling them foodstuffs are also subject to the death penalty

This is a categorical warning to the non-Jewish population against:

1) Providing shelter to Jews,
2) Supplying them with food,
3) Selling them foodstuffs.

Częstochowa 9 24 42
#20 https://en.wikipedia.org/wiki/History_of_the_Jews_in_20 th-century-Poland

I can easily recall the unannounced, rough searches. The hanging on the door in the middle of the night was not a knocking, it was a relentless pounding. I was fast asleep under my toasty down comforter, my *perineh*, a remnant of my other unmentionable home long ago. *"Aufmachen!"* (Open up!) the voice thundered. *Matka* had no choice but to allow the two high-booted soldiers into the house.

Two gigantic men, seemingly as tall as trees to me, were in front of me, directing a flashlight at my head. I could see the tops of their leather boots. One of them passed the light over my hair, my nose, my whole face. Then the other grabbed my chin, roughly turning my head. I was wide awake now. He shined the light into my eyes. My hand, still warm from my *perineh*, rubbed my eyes, as my breathing slowed. Could they hear my beating heart?

"Jude! Jude!" The shrill voice shouted. Whatever did that mean? Gentleness toward a sleeping child was not part of their vocabulary. Only the presence of *Matka* standing there in her frayed, green pajamas kept me from panic. I was choked up inside. I could not make my throat utter a sound!

"*Gucia, moja kochana,* show the soldiers how you say your prayers." A shivering *Matka* seemed to be pleading with me.

I wasn't moving quickly enough. "Schnell! Mach schnell!" One of the booted men pulled the cover off me, as I lay there curled up with my knees to my chest. He grabbed my shoulders, and suddenly I was standing on the icy floor. For a split second, I caught a glimpse of *Jezus Christus*, his long hair, his gentle smile and familiar face which had been a comfort to me before. *Matka* repeated herself softly, forcing a faint smile, and looking directly into my disbelieving eyes. "Gucia, show the gentlemen how *well* you can say your prayers."

My toe hit against the gray pail standing at the foot of the bed. It was my toilet, so I wouldn't have to go outside in the night frost. I would have welcomed that at this moment. A third time *Matka* said something, this time to the soldiers. "She's Christian. My granddaughter. You'll see."

My trembling knees thumped down on the icy wood floor. My palms touched each other. My dark, crossed eyes roamed the beautifully draped, serene face above my bed, the face that seemed to calm me. Then I began, tentatively, the Polish prayer to the Holy Mother Mary *(Matka Boska).*

"*Zdrowaś Maryjo, Iaski pelna, Pan z Tobą, blogoslawionaś Ty między niewiastami, i blogoslawiony owoc żywota Twojego, Jezus . . .* [Hail Mary, full of Grace, the Lord is with thee. Blessed art thou amongst women, and blessed is the Fruit of thy womb, Jesus . . .]." (Cit. 21)

The men shut the flashlight, snapped their heels, and walked out. Had our family's assimilation, my brothers going to a Polish public school, speaking Polish in the house, not Yiddish, helped me to remain in this nest? Perhaps. They found no *Juden* in this house that night.

I still wonder if I really fooled them. Did they actually think I was a Polish, Christian child? Or did they possibly discern that I wasn't, but perhaps one of them had their own little girl, or a baby sister, and that recognition stayed their evil hand, allowing me to live. How did they know which house to search? Had someone, in the hopes of getting two pounds of sugar, and the victim's clothing, betrayed Maria Kowalczyk and told them she was hiding a Jewish child? But they found no *Juden* living in that house that night.

Today I am also pondering the veracity of my stated relationship to *Matka*. In front of the soldiers, she introduced me as her granddaughter. While Stanka did have German boyfriends, would Marianna, in fervently Catholic Poland, admit that I was her illegitimate grandchild? On the other hand, translations indicate she took me to her neighbors for chitchat and told them I was the daughter of her widowed cousin from Borzych. Who was I really? I was told to call her *Matka*, but she was about forty-six years old when I was four, a bit too old to have such a young child at that time. Perhaps I was just imitating Stanka because she called her *matka*. More puzzles. But I never asked questions. Just followed directions.

One day, *Matka* dressed me in a beautiful white dress. Marilyn Starr told me that Stanka made that dress for me out of curtains. She put ribbons of many colors on my head. And I danced in that dress. I danced to *The Sailor's Dance* by Rinehart Glier. My hands were placed on my waist and my toes pointed to left and right alternately with each leg and a skip hop in between. Whenever I hear that music today, I am tempted to perform that little dance. I think the white dress was actually a first communion outfit. This was another way Maria Kowalczyk, my saintly *Matka*, strove to protect me.

In the spring and summer, I meandered in the garden among the cherry trees and flowers. I picked the plump, dark red cherries from the tree and the fully ripened ones fallen on the ground, and ate them, ignoring the red juices trickling down my lips and chin. I have never, since, tasted the luscious flavor or essence of this fruit from those fresh cherries right off the tree. I've eaten cherry Lifesavers, cough drops, cherry jam, cherry pie, cherry Jell-O, cherry ice cream, maraschino cherries, and even regular cherries, but none have ever tasted like those.

There were also yellow, saucer-like sunflowers growing by the side of the house. They were my measuring devices in that garden. *Matka* would determine my growth on the thick sunflower stems. "Look how big you got, Gucia!" She'd exclaim. There were many songbirds attracted to those sunflowers, including this little *przepiorka*. Flowers also substituted for toys I never had and helped to entertain me.

I would often pick the wild flowers by the side of the dirt road and take them to her.

"*Matka*, some flowers I picked for you."

"Oh, I love them," she smiled as she put her arm around me and squeezed me tightly. "Especially the purple ones. Let's do something with them. Let's make crowns."

She held up a purple flower to my nose. "Smell it, Gucia. How sweet."

We sat on the cool grass, my legs apart and extended in front of me. The flowers were strewn in the V of my outstretched bony legs. Yellow, purple, pink, and white ones.

"I will make a crown for you. Can you show me how?"

"Here, like this." She began to braid the stems, and then took my fingers to loosely insert the purple among the other colors. My fingers fumbled at first, but eventually I succeeded, producing a somewhat fragile but colorful product.

"*Matka*, here's your crown."

"*Djenkuye* [Thank you]. Now we'll make one for you, Gucia, *moja kochana.*" (My dear)

When I was not making flower crowns and had to be indoors, I was taught to spin yarn on the spinning wheel. Since Maria Kowalczyk was reputed to have made the warmest gloves in Wegrow, she had to have a spinning wheel. That proved to be another form of entertainment for me. No children to play with, just solitary activities with my *Matka*.

One gorgeous summer day, I was in the garden with Stanka, *Matka's* beautiful blonde daughter. Two German soldiers, tall and erect, entered the garden. Their boots were almost as high as my waist, and on their uniform, there were peculiar looking bent crosses. They spoke in a foreign tongue. Stanka suggested, "Gucia, show the gentlemen how you sing and dance." And they echoed, "Sing for us, dance for us. We'll give you *tzukerki*" (candy). Candy was, of course, a popular extrinsic reward for a four- or five-year-old.

But how did I react to their entrance? What signals of fear did my body give me? I do remember obliging them, but what song did I sing? Did I get my feet to move in rhythm? What did I dance to? Did I falter? How did the candy taste? Their taste was certainly not as memorable as the cherries on that tree in that distant, long ago garden. I sang for the sweet *tsukerki* and danced, to live another day, to measure my tomorrows on the sunflowers.

In a Distant Garden

> I remember the cherries on the tree
> In that distant, long ago garden,
> Their sweetness, juiciness, their "cherriness."
> The sunflower was my yardstick
> Of my yesterdays and tomorrows.
> There was sunshine on my face,
> Sunflowers in the garden.
> The two entered so erectly,
> Boots glinting in the sunlight,
> On their arms the crooked cross
> Seemed made of bent, blunt crowbars.
> There was sunshine on my face,

Sunflowers in the garden.
And then they asked me
To sing for them, to dance,
Dance for your life, they seemed to say
And sing to live another day
To measure inches on sunflower stems,
Sunshine on your face,
Sunflowers in your garden.
I don't remember dancing feet
To get the sweet *tzukerki,*
Not sweet, but sawdust on my dappled tongue,
And stains upon my singing heart.
So I could live another day
To measure more tomorrows
On the sunflowers in that garden.

There was loud noise, bombing very close to my sixth birthday. The Russians were possibly bombing Siedlice, only about five miles from Wegrow. I remember a space the opposite of a sunny garden, an underground space at the far end of a potato field where we had to live as those bombs were falling. I very recently learned that, not too far away, another little girl about my age, Lusia Farbiarz, also had to live underground. She was one of four children who had survived out of the 11,000 Wegrow ghetto population. Her house had been destroyed in stages by the bombing, first doors and windows, and then the entire house. Because she was sick with a temperature, she needed to be fed and kept warm, so her "matka" (rescuer), Pelagia Vogelgezang, also went underground into a pit that she and her husband had dug.

I remember a damp, dark, cramped space about ten by fourteen feet and five and one-fourth feet high. It was high enough for me to stand in, but *Matka* had to bend her knees or her neck in order to keep her head from banging into its dusty, crumbly ceiling. *Matka,*

Stanka, and I each had our designated space to sleep on on the damp, hard ground of the pit in the potato field where we lived for a period of time before the end of the war, while planes and bombs were roaring over Poland.

It smelled of earth; the odor an earthworm might know if it had nostrils, as it worked its way underground. Only very loud noises penetrated down into it. We could hear the noise of planes jetting overhead. They sounded as though they were flying ten feet above our heads. Occasionally, there was a frightful blast that sounded like a bomb exploding. But more ordinary sounds of people walking nearby, talking in normal voices, a horse and buggy passing on an adjacent dirt road, children playing hop scotch, a boy on his bicycle on the nearby path—we couldn't hear these sounds clearly.

I had a thin sheet spread out, my pillow, and my warm *perineh*. I would roll myself in it so some of it was under me, adding some warmth and softness. *Matka* had her pillow, blanket, and a thin sheet on the ground in one corner. I never saw *Matka* actually lie down on hers, but I remember myself sleeping there and eating there in the pit, like Lusia. I clearly remember potatoes.

Matka would leave the pit, go into the house, cook the potatoes and bring them back into the pit for me to eat. Boiled potatoes, with a little salt. How delicious they tasted! *Matka* ate some, and Stanka did, too, when she was down there with us. I always got the largest portion.

One day, *Matka* went out to get some potatoes from the field. We waited and waited for her to return. The planes were flying very low. We heard gunshots and bombs. She must have been out several hours. It seemed like an endless day. As I looked out from the entrance hole, I noticed a gray, sunless sky. After all, we lived in a potato field. There was no shortage of potatoes. Why was it taking so long?

I began to fidget. It was dark. It was cold. Where were my potatoes? I moved my tongue around in my salivating mouth, practically feeling the potatoes' grainy texture and their salty taste. Not only did she get the potatoes, but she must have cooked them by now, I thought. They would be soothingly hot to my shivering body. Finally! I saw her feet first. Her black, laced, shoes, all muddy, were lowering themselves into the pit. Sure, I was happy to see her, but my first thought was, *Now I can eat.*

I had never seen my *Matka* look like that. Her face was smeared with dirt, and the whole front of her apron and dress were caked with mud. She took breaths between her words. She was holding *two* filthy potatoes, one in each hand. Raw potatoes. What happened? She explained:

"There was shooting…I was in the field. I got down on my stomach. I was all the way at the other end of the potato field. I crawled on my stomach the entire way. It took so much time… Two raw potatoes. Maybe tomorrow…"

Eventually the planes and the shooting and the explosions stopped. We resurfaced from the pit into the house. Wegrow was liberated by the Russians in August 1944.

The war in Europe was over May 8, 1945. I could now go to school. I had a new little schoolbag that I could carry on my shoulder. And my red and white dress, though getting too short, still fit. I had good leather shoes (perhaps my father had made them years before) and knee socks. Perfect for the first day of school. *Matka* had a bow ready for my hair. She put both her index fingers on top of my hair and curled it around her fingers as she did each Sunday for church. But since I had not started my education at the appropriate age, I had to catch up. At six and a half years of age, I did not even know my alphabet, and reading seemed so far beyond my reach.

Matka kept practicing the letters with me. She told me the letter, then the sound. She gave me simple words. I stayed up much too late and cried tears of frustration and fear. I don't remember exactly how long it took, but *Matka's* patience cemented it for me. The smile on her face seemed as broad as her shoulders when I got it right!

She herself had probably not been educated beyond third grade, so she was a perfect candidate to be a slave for the Reich, no education needed. But she was a consummate and patient teacher. I must have been a quick and successful learner, for I remember the teacher calling on me to read, and exclaiming: "If she can do it, why can't the rest of you!" Perhaps, at school, I would have children to play with.

I noticed some children who had not prepared their homework, or because of other school infractions, sitting in the back of the room with weights on their shoulders. Or they were made to sit on a tall stool with a pointed hat, a dunce cap on their head. I did not want to be one of those kids. I never was.

CHAPTER 7

AUNT NORMA

One day, while in the kitchen with *Matka*, there was a tapping on the door. There stood a woman with a gaunt, pale face. On her head she wore a flowered kerchief, covering most of her frizzy, brown hair. She was thin and had dark bags under her eyes. She looked a bit familiar. Then she shouted a word I hadn't heard in more than three years! "Gitele!" she exclaimed with tears glistening as she hugged me! She was my Aunt Norma, my father's youngest sister! How different she looked. *Matka*, wiping her hands on her apron, exclaimed, "Norma Przepiorka, *tak!*" (Yes) For a few moments, I was confused. We were all speechless, just looking at each other, Norma sobbing. *(My father's customer, Thomashevsky, whom she had met after jumping off the train, told her In Yiddish: *"Mendl's tochter lebt."* Mendl's daughter is alive. That's how Norma knew I had survived.)

"This I brought for you, a doll and a little carriage!" Real toys! As exciting as this was, I had no way of knowing what an important role this aunt was to play in the saga of my fractured life. Later I learned that Aunt Norma had escaped the hell fire by jumping off a stalled train bound for the death camp Treblinka. Her husband was shot. Norma knew that her brother, my Uncle Fishl, was hidden in a basement freezer room (where huge blocks of ice were kept) at Edick Butchinsky's. When Norma jumped off the train, she went to the woman for whom they had sewed clothes, Pania Biernatzka, looking to be hidden by her. This lady knew about Fishl at Butchinsky's and directed Norma to them.

Butchinsky had a restaurant in a suburban part of Wegrow, Rozbitche, and that is where he kept my Uncle Fishl, hiding him in the ice cellar. Butchinsky was also one of the righteous people who had to live in fear, hide, and probably lie to his neighbors. He was also hiding ten-year-old Sara Nortman, who survived the ghetto's liquidation. She was one of the four children who survived of the 100 or so total number of survivors of the Wegrow ghetto. See below.

Researchers estimate that between 100 and 157 Wegrow Jews are thought to have survived, and among them, two to four children.

> No more than one hundred of Wegrow's Jews are thought to have survived the war. Some did so, by making their way to Mordy to join a forced labor camp, at which Jews continued to work. Most of the remainder of Wegrow's Jews depended on the assistance of local Poles. Several young children were taken into the homes of Polish families. These included *Gitel Przepiorka*, a three-year-old when her mother turned her over to the Kowalczyks in the summer of 1942; *Zofia Shenberg*, an abandoned infant discovered by Marianna Ruszkowska in Wegrow on Yom Kippur 1942; *Lusia Fabiarz* found by Pelagia Vogelgesang on May 1, 1943; and ten-year-old *Sara Nortman* who survived the ghetto's liquidation by living with the Buczynski family. Source #22

Norma hid behind a door in the vestibule for two hours, as many Germans were eating there. Then she went down to see her brother, Fishl, who suffered from kidney disease. He died very close to liberation. She lamented that she had to bury him with her own hands.

After the war, Aunt Norma was going to a DP (Displaced Persons) Camp called Foerhenwald, in Germany. She said the Poles were still killing Jews, so here she hoped to be helped by American soldiers administering the camp to find her older sister, Esther Bernstein living in NY since the 1920s. She wanted to notify her she was alive, and I, too, was alive. Perhaps Esther and her husband Max might bring us to America. So Norma would soon be on her way to a new place. And so would I, though I did not yet know it. She spoke some words to my *Matka* and to me, words I don't recall. Was this going to be another abrupt separation from a loved one? She left so quickly. But I did have some reason to hope, because she made me believe we would see each other again. I actually remember visiting her in Foehrenwald and seeing her serve chicken soup! But *Matka* didn't want Norma to take me with her. For clarification, it is important to cite a very significant experience Norma had in Foehrenwald.

How my few remaining relatives in Europe and the U.S. learned of my survival is a tale of pure luck and serendipity. Foehrenwald was located in the Southwestern part of Germany, close to the Swiss border. Very soon after its founding, Jewish religious life was revitalized there. In spite of crowded conditions and the poor health of many, these people were reborn. The bleak surroundings didn't deter the survivors from initiating self-governing practices, and social and cultural activities, and repairing their broken lives to the best of their abilities. I believe the outlook might have been: "You're alone, I'm alone. Let's be alone together." Many of those marriages lasted over fifty years! And the birth rate was the highest in the world at that time! It was in this atmosphere of looking forward, and without any other means to locate her family in the United States, that my Aunt Norma, in a large room filled with other survivors and some American soldiers, decided to make her strategic move. She wanted to notify her older sister, Esther, who lived in New York, that she and I were alive. Aunt Norma spoke Polish and Yiddish, the language of many Eastern European Jews, and she knew not a word of English, the language of the American soldiers. But she hoped names were possibly the same in all languages. So, palpably agitated, with her hazel eyes darting to all corners of the room, she shouted: "Esther, Max, Bernstein, Bronx, New York! Esther, Max, Bernstein, Bronx, New York!"

Silence descended on the room. People gave each other questioning looks. "*Ver is dos? Vos teet zie?* (Who is that? What is she doing?)" Norma kept looking around. Was there someone here from New York? Could he help her find her older sister?

A tall, dark-haired American soldier, Phil Kaplan, approaches her and looks at her in disbelief. He speaks to her in his broken Yiddish. He is the neighbor of Esther and Max Bernstein on Wythe Place in the Bronx! And their son, Sam, her nephew and my cousin, was his best friend! He immediately sends a telegram to his mother telling her Mrs. Bernstein's sister, and her little niece are alive. Two of the lost had been found. The only two of about seventy.

Esther sent a ship ticket on the *Ernie Pyle* to Phil Kaplan. Norma came to the United States in 1947. In the meantime, *Matka*, so able with needle and thread, made me a new coat and hat. "We are going on a trip," she revealed. I made sure to bring my new treasured toys, my doll and carriage, and we were soon in a place called *Jelonia Gura* (yellow mountain), where a huge windmill enchanted me. This still puzzles me. Why couldn't I also come in 1947 with Norma?

I didn't realize 'til much later how much my *Matka* had grown to love me. She had promised my mother, now a young widow, that if I survived and someone from my biological family came to claim me, she would give me up to them. But what was she doing now? She was taking me to a remote and unfamiliar place, hoping that perhaps no one would find me there. I also found out more recently that the mill had been owned by the Friedman family, whom she also had hidden in her barn and rescued.

While we explored the mill, I saw *Matka* covered in the white powder many times, as the flour ground there covered her clothes. She slapped her hands together and tousled my hair to get the excess flour out of it when I emerged a gray-haired six-year old! Norma wanted to take me to America. Why didn't she? There were multiple reasons—some practical, some emotional, why Matka didn't want me to go to America with Norma. *Jelonia Gora* was less anti-Semitic, and she still was concerned about my safety in Wegrow. She also saw that Norma had a new husband and a newborn daughter to care for and had not the means to take on another child's welfare. *Matka* also knew that my Aunt Esther and Uncle Max were rich and could afford to give me a fine education and a comfortable life. And emotionally, she was very attached to me and was hoping nobody would find me there and that I could stay with her forever.

There was also remuneration from the Coordinating Committee for the Rescue of Jewish Children. And survivor families registered with this organization to find their children and get them back from their Christian rescuers. Marilyn Starr confided in me that Maria Kowalczyk was cheated and not fully paid. How dare they do that! What she had done was priceless!

But another unfamiliar and unexpected place awaited me, one I don't even recall being in.

I was watching the windmill go round and round when two men drove up in what to me looked like a box on wheels. I had never seen a car. There had been only two cars in the town of Wegrow, one owned by a doctor, and the other by a Polish nobleman. The men spoke to my *Matka* words I could not hear. These two men were actually sent by my Aunt Esther after she got the message from her neighbor Phil Kaplan who had met Aunt Norma, and they were sent by the War Orphans Project in conjunction with The Canadian Jewish Congress and UNRRA (United Nations Relief and Rehabilitation Administration), which helped to find Jewish surviving orphans. Esther and Max Bernstein wanted to expedite my arrival in the United States. So they paid for private agents to find me and accompany me on this journey.

Before I knew it, these people were offering me an adventure-filled ride in this four-wheeled contraption, with delicious snacks of chocolate and cookies. "I'll come if *Matka* comes too," I declared. Was I too distracted to notice my *Matka's* eyes were welling up and her face turning pale? She was about to lose this child she had succored and grown to love so deeply. Or was *Matka* thinking, *But finally Gucia was going to her own family. This is where she belongs, isn't it? I have to keep my promise. I will always remember her. Perhaps she'll visit.*

I was forcefully removed by these strangers, two men and a woman, without even a proper goodbye. I never saw my *Matka* again. *Matka* never saw me again. The immediately ensuing events were dim and blurry.

CHAPTER 8

FROM HOME TO HOME

I found myself at a small airport, in Wroclaw, where my *Matka* took me, did *Matka* go with me, and then when I scratched woman's face, was that at the airport? When I asked her how she got them, she said a cat had done it. This must have been quite a while after she got them, because Marianna Kowalczyk's testimony indicated I ran off the plane back to her, screaming, "Mother, don't let them take me away!" That woman with the scratched face was Mrs. Allberg, (later Janina Kowalska), and I was the cat. This parting occurred on July 18, 1945, when I was six years old. I was on my way to the next stop of my long journey to America, but there was an interim stop, a place called *Dom Dziecka* (children's home) in Otwock, Poland. The documents from the Jewish Historical Institute relate to that parting, including registration, my aunt Esther's financial status, my Aunt Norma's wanting to take me, and included my last address before the Otwock home as being Brzeska 19, Warsawa, probably Mrs. Allberg's address.

Marianna Kowalczyk's statement says I didn't get there just then. I remember being in an apartment with a family for a few days. Perhaps I was so upset that Mrs. Allberg had to take me to her own home to calm me down, because the orphanage, founded and run by survivors, could not accept a wild and screaming child. I am thinking that behavior could upset some of the orphans there whose experiences were more harrowing than mine.

My separation from my *Matka* was so traumatic that I totally wiped a whole year out of my life and my mind. I didn't want to be there! This orphanage's philosophy stressed education and Jewish culture, such as leading a little band or orchestra, and singing, so that its young residents were given many opportunities to get back to normal and peaceful lives and forget some of their traumatic experiences. The food was very good there, and so was the education. I was described by the Canadian Jewish Archives as doing well in second grade primary school, but also being a non-participant in any of these amusements provided there. What's more, it is really strange how I found this information. It all came about from the word "chubby," which was a description of me in the papers relating to the Canadian War Orphans Project.

I have in my possession two little pictures of myself. One was taken in June of 1945 by Szpielman (the go-to photographer) in Wegrow. That is the one *Matka* had dressed me up for and had me send to my Aunt Esther right after the war, before I left Esther, to show her I survived. My thin face and bony knees definitely would not lead anyone to describe me as chubby. During wartime, no one in Poland had enough food to eat.

The second picture I have is of my face only, possibly a passport picture. Here my face does look a bit fuller. When I turned the picture over, I saw the name of a town, Otwock. I looked up Otwock and learned it is the hometown of Irena Sendler (1910–2008), the Polish humanitarian who saved thousands of Jewish children during the Holocaust. But another significant fact caught my eye. There was a children's home, *Dom Dziecka* (orphanage), founded there after the war by a woman named Franciszka Oliva, with the help of Russian commander of a Soviet Field Hospital. This converted slum-like building on 11 Boleslaw Prusa Street became a home for about 130 child survivors. Wide-eyed and open-mouthed, I saw myself in a group picture there, sitting among the little residents on the ground!

I am in front row, third from right on the ground (with glasses).

Cit. #23

I don't remember having friends, playing with anyone, or having an attachment to a specific person. But from the visuals about the home, and my own picture, it is clear that we, the children, were very well entertained, educated and well fed. I actually look chubby! I do remember here, bins of clothing, probably arranged by size, where I could pick out a set number of items. I was only about seven and my size probably changed frequently.

#24
http://www.yadvashem.org/yv/en/exhibitions/otwock/hom e.asp
"Most of the educators and staff were also Holocaust survivors,
who saw in their work a sense of mission and destiny, an
answer to the loss they had experienced in the Holocaust…"

The Joint Distribution Committee financially supported the children's home. After 1947 their financial support was reduced and at the end of 1949, when there were only 52 children remaining, it was officially closed." Cit. #25 I was at this orphanage for about fifteen months but had completely blocked it out of my memory. I didn't want to be there. I wanted only to be with *Matka!* Can you just picture the scene of a breathless six -year-old little girl screaming and wailing, trying to get back to her sobbing "mother" on a runway! There I was, with my curly mop of hair bouncing, my wet, crossed eyes, and my ill-fitting glasses almost falling off, running out of a plane where I am the only passenger!

Running Out of a Plane (A Poem) January 9, 2018 based on Maria Kowalczyk's testimony

A mother, a child, a runway, a plane,
A runaway child,
To a mother, a *matka*, a savior, a saint
The child runs, screams, keens, begs
Breathless, fearless, frightened, bravely yelling
to the only mother she remembers.
Mother number two, I want to be with you!
You, who loved me, saved me.
I want to make flower crowns,
To measure my yesterdays, on sunflower stems,
In that distant, long-ago garden.
Mother, mother, where are they taking me?
Don't let them take me away,
Don't let them
Don't
Good bye. Forever.

By Gloria Glantz January 9, 2018

Illustration by my seven-year old granddaughter, Lexi Glantz

A chronological summary of the events after Wegrow liberation April 22, 1945, and end of WWII on May 8, 1945, and my journey out of Poland to two more institutions in a different country, Sweden.

- About April 7, 1945, Norma applied to take me to Foehrenwald. I visited there.
- Between April 7 and July 18, 1945 these events were described in Maria Kowalczyks own handwriting.
- On July 8, 1945, I was picked up in a car with two men and a woman, Mrs. Allberg, to go to Dom Dziecka in Otwock.
- On August 10, 1945, I was registered at *Dom Dziecka.*
- Between July 8 and August 10, I stayed with Mrs. Allberg (twenty-two days) as my last address on the registration is her address.

I stayed at *Dom Dziecka* from August 10, 1945 to November 1946, as the last address is also Mrs. Allberg's.

- September 19, 1946—A special emissary is awaiting me in Sweden.
- October 15, 1946—Application for my passport is made.
- October 21, 1946—Mrs. Allberg receives my passport, enabling me to go to Sweden.
- November 1946—I leave Dom Dziecka for Sweden
- November 1946 to January 1947—It was possible I stayed at Foehrenwald with Aunt Norma because documents indicate I remember staying with my aunt and then an orphanage in Poland. I remember being there, but probably life there was not extraordinary in any way and I was safe with an aunt, so I don't remember any other activities than seeing her serve her chicken soup. I do have a vague memory that I also, helped her serve the chicken soup to some persons there.
- January 1947 to April 1947—I went to the *Mosaiska Forsamlingen* home, run by the JDC (Joint Distribution Committee) and UNRRA. See Sweden section
- April 1947 to December 1947—I was transferred to Fiskeby-Vardhem, the Lutheran Orphanage in Sweden. I remember this one a bit better. (See Sweden)

The above information is from the translated documents of *The Jewish Historical Institute,* (Anna Przybyszewska Drozd) and a file from the *Canadian Jewish Congress Archives* (Adara Goldberg) #25 JHI # 26 Adara,

I became a stranger once again.

I remember Marilyn Starr (nee Maryla Friedman) saying that Stanka might have been running after my airplane. It's possible Stanka did accompany me to the airport as I left the Kowalczyks for Otwock children's home. The woman with the scratches on her face, the UNRRA representative, was with me on a small plane before I ran off of it.

Looking back now I see I had no control of my destiny. No options, no choices. Again ripped away from those I loved. Is life like this considered a life well lived? I was seething with internal turmoil. Will it ever be different? Will life ever be mine, not what has been thrust upon me? Once again, the little bird had to fly away and leave the warm nest.

CHAPTER 9

REGRETS AND REPENTANCE

W henever I give testimony about this time in my life, I am always asked if I ever went back to see *Matka*.

I never returned to see her. When I arrived in Montreal at age eight, I wanted to write to her. But my Montreal family discouraged it. "Forget your past. That was another time. You are here now. We don't have her address." The prevailing thinking at that time was to look forward, not backward. Today, in an electronic age, I believe the philosophy would be different.

I tried to write to her when I arrived in New York at age twelve. I got the same reasoning. This was always a deep regret and a hole in my soul, that I never thanked her for her love and care, and for the courage to risk her life to save me. I did eventually find a way to partially heal that deep hurt inside me, which I will describe in a later chapter. And I did get the opportunity to at least ask her forgiveness.

By the time I entered high school, that desire to communicate with my Polish mother was again ignited. By now I had some very close friends with whom I had shared my complete background. The question was always the same: Did you ever contact her? And the answer was also the same—no.

In the late 1970s, my cousin from Israel, Ephraim Przepiorka, whom we affectionately called Fishl (Uncle Shlomo's son), visited us. He had left his parents in the 1920s to become a Chalutz, (a pioneer) in Palestine, now Israel. He had been part of the committee that wrote a memorial book about my birth town, Wegrow. Consequently, he had communicated with a few survivors of our town and had interesting information for me. He told me that he knew of a family in New Jersey, the Friedman family, one of whom was also hidden by this same woman, Maria Kowalczyk. I was excited.

We were invited to their home one Sunday, and they showed a slide of her at around age eighty, a face I did not remember or recognize. But they also said they had visited her and she still had an oil painting of me on her wall! She had even asked them if they might try to discover, in their crowd of guests at their daughter Michelle's upcoming wedding, anyone who might know what had happened to Chanushah, as she referred to me. I grabbed this unforeseen opportunity.

I took pictures of my own family, and since I had lost my Polish language ability, asked them to send these pictures and tell her I was well, always remembered her, and thanked her from the bottom of my heart for her courage and kindness during that terrible time. They agreed to do that.

Some years later, in May of 1990, there was a large international gathering of hidden children in New York City. I found a picture of us at that meeting. Also, Elie Wiesel was there. I attended with my family and anxiously awaited the arrival of the Friedmans to ask them about my communication to Pania Kowalczyk. We met and I got crushing news.

They told me they hadn't written to her because, they explained, it would make her feel worse since I hadn't written all those years. Though they made that decision for me without consulting me, I did understand their reasoning. In the meantime, she had died. I was devastated! I should have taken the responsibility of contacting the Polish embassy or found another Polish-speaking source and had that letter written. I now even could get her address!

I was racked with guilt for not taking that responsibility and making sure she got the letter. I could not stop thinking about this missed opportunity.

In 2005, I saw a film titled *Hidden Children and Their Rescuers* produced by Aviva Slesin, also a hidden child. Watching it, I became tearful in many spots, especially where the survivors had connected with their long-ago rescuers. I saw their tears of joy and gratitude. But one of the clips in that movie went straight to my gut was when a beautiful, blonde rescuer, visibly emotional and sobbing, was expressing herself in a most articulate and honest way. The film depicted a little boy she had sheltered, who was found and claimed by his surviving father. "Yes," she sobbed, "his father had every right to take his son. That was his right. But did he have to cut us, who had loved him and cared for him, off completely?"

Her question opened a cavernous hole of regret in me. I suddenly saw my *Matka* in the days, weeks, and months after I was taken from her. What, I reflected, could she have been thinking on that day?

Was there anything I could do to remove the weight off my heart? Or at least to shrink it?

On *Yom Kippur* afternoon of 2007, Renee Edelman, the rabbi of my congregation gave certain biblical passages for comment to various members of the congregation. I was offered one from *Pirkei Avot (Wisdom of the Fathers)*: *Bamakom she ein anashim hishtadel lihiot eesh.* #27 "In a place where there is no humanity, strive to be human." That fit. *Matka* personified it. My speech follows.

If There Was a Moment I Could Change

When the "box on wheels," what most kids would call a car, arrived in Yelena Gura, instead of being six, I wish I had been fifteen. By then I might have been more mature, thoughtful, not selfish or self-involved. I would have been sad leaving, yes, but I would have said the proper good-bye to my Polish *Matka* knowing I was going to my actual biological family. I would have understood. What would the proper good-bye have been?

We could have had some conversation. I would have asked her some questions. How long did it take me to call you "*Matka*?" What kind of child was I? Did I talk about my original family to you? You were so patient when I was learning my alphabet. I cried and tried.

You encouraged me patiently, made me repeat the letters, and rejoiced with a big smile when I learned them. You made me feel loved. What made you love me so? I remember you teaching me the prayers to the *Matka Boska* so I would sound like a good Catholic child. You even had me say these prayers in front of the German soldiers who held a flashlight to my face in the middle of the night. What made you so astute about guiding my behavior in front of those enemy soldiers?

I would have looked into her eyes and explained why I considered myself a miracle wrought by her. Perhaps by then I might have known about the red-headed little Worim girl who lived in a non-Jewish neighborhood, didn't look Jewish, and was outside playing when her parents were rounded up for Treblinka (*Last Jew of Wegrow*, p. 94, citation #28). When she was seen wandering around helplessly at night, she was reported by her neighbors so the Germans could pick her up by her legs and shatter her head against the concrete wall. I could have been such a little girl.

"What did you do not to have your neighbors betray me?" I would have asked her. "What did you tell them? What influenced you? Didn't you know you could be killed? Thank you sounds so inadequate for what you accomplished. But thank you is all I have." I would have said, "Thank you for your kindness, for your patience, for your good sense, for your affection, your sacrifice, your risk-taking, your love—for my life. Thank you for being a mother to me. I will not ever forget you. I will make your name known so others will always recognize your heroism and your goodness!"

If I could change one thing, I would have gone back to visit her when I was an adult. I would have sent her money if she needed it. How deeply I regret never having contacted her all those years! I was so busy "becoming" more normal, less fearful, Canadian, American. I was becoming a child, a teenager. The psychology of the time was: *Move on. Don't dwell on the past! Forget the past. Be here now.* When I wanted to write to you, I was given the standard excuses. "We don't have her address." "You have to go on with your life." "That was in the past, forget about it." "You're here now." Why didn't they let me write to you? What harm would it have done? I don't remember my reaction to their reasoning. But I wasn't forceful enough. I should have insisted! I should have had tantrums. On the other hand, I was obedient. I always had to be polite. I couldn't disobey, remember? There was so much forgetting. Each day I was blossoming, learning, feeling, growing, catching up.

What thoughts could *she* have had on the day I was taken from her so abruptly? Did she think, Gucia, moja kochana, *how I will miss you! I know I made a promise to your own* Matka *and papa. Your father was good to us. How could I know I would grow to love you so deeply! I did not think of the danger to my family and me when I took you. I only knew it was the right and Christian thing to do. I will look for your shining dark eyes, full head of black curls, your little dancing feet, your sweet voice singing. Who will make crowns of flowers for me now! I will always pray to our Lord, Jesus, for your safety. Do not forget me. Will I ever see you again?*

If I could change one thing, it would be to never have had such causes to regret.

On *Yom Kippur*, we are exhorted to seek forgiveness of those we have willfully or accidentally wronged. I never contacted my Polish *Matka*, never told her about my new life, never asked how she was after I left her, and never thanked her for risking her life to save me. In a place where little humanity could be found, she climbed the highest summit of humanity and heroism. In front of this distinguished congregation of friends, neighbors and family, I now ask her forgiveness.

Matka, your god is not my god; whither you went, I did not go. Your people were not my people. The Book of Ruth (negation of Ruth's speech to Naomi, Ruth 1:16) citation # 29 But you gave me life a third time. You are my hero. I wish I could have seen you after my name was no longer Gucia. I wish I could have kissed your feet for giving me life a third time. Please forgive me, *moja kochana Matka*. In a place where no one behaves like a human being, you must strive to be human. You are a shining example of what it is to be human.

Bamakom sheein anashim, hishtadel lihiot eesh.

You knew your *Hillel, Matka*. You wrought miracles.

The pictures below at the end of the chapter.

1. I am in a carriage, my brothers behind me, parents on left, Aunt Norma next to me and other aunts and uncles. The man in a bowtie is cousin Fishl, who left for Palestine the next day, August 31, 1939. Germans enter Poland September 1, 1939 #1

2. Craig at Treblinka on March of the Living trip

3. Mother, Estera Przepiorka
4. Brother, Yitzchak Przepiorka
5. Brother, Zelig Przepiorka, with required armband
6. Gitl Przepiorka, about to become Chanusha Gucia Kowalczyk, age about three and a half (at *Matka's*)
7. Father, Mendl Przepiorka

8. Chanusha Gucia Kowalczyk, professionally posed picture to be remembered by, taken June 20, 1945 in Wegrow, Poland (Also sent to Aunt Esther on Wythe Place in the Bronx, with a note from me) according to Maria Kowalczyk

9. Passport picture of Gucia Przepiorka, seven years old, Otwock Children's home before going to Sweden

10. Aunt Sarah and my father, Mendl
11. Uncle Avraham
12. Uncle Shlomo and Aunt Esther Braindl (taken August 1939)—
    Fishl's parents
13. My family in our summer country home, Jarnic. Yitzchak has
    two dogs near him.

16   17

14. *Matka* and Gucia before getting separated; maybe school beginning
15. Gucia with doll from Aunt Norma
16. Aunt Norma's travel documents on Ernie Pyle
17. Aunt Norma and Uncle Willie (her second husband) in Fohrenwald DP camp
    Segue into transition of going to Sweden.

DOCUMENTS FOR
PART I - POLAND

In Maria Kowalcyzk's own handwriting where she claims my town's living conditions were average, and in another document, she says Wegrow conditions were very anti-Semitic even after the war, but in Jelonia Gora they were better.

From Polish Historical Institute received October 30, 2017

11. Czy był aresztowany(a), szantażowany(a), siedział(a) w więzieniu, obozie _____

12. Utrzymywał(a) się z funduszów: własnych, krewnych, przyjaciół — żydów, nie-żydów ( ), społecznych, innych _____

13. Czy posiada jakieś dokumenty (fotografie, pamiętniki, zapiski, dane statystyczne itp.) dotyczące martyrologii żydów, czy pragnie opowiedzieć lub opisać swoje przeżycia _____

14. Krewni, którzy przebywali w Polsce 1.IX.39 i ocaleli

NAZWISKO I IMIĘ	WIEK	STOPIEŃ POKREWIEŃSTWA	OBECNY ADRES

15. Krewni zagranicą

NAZWISKO I IMIĘ	STOPIEŃ POKREWIEŃSTWA	KRAJ POBYTU

16. Uwagi *panna* _____ *ojciec zmarł* _____

17. Adres dla korespondencji (ew. nazwisko przybrane i zmiany adresu) _____

KOMITET w _____   Data _____

Podpis urzędnika   Podpis rejestrującego się

H. M./M. S.   Druk. St. Winiarski, Targowa 25.

JHI, received October 30, 2017

A B C D E F G H I J K L Ł M N O P R S T U W Z Ż

Centralny Komitet Żydów Polskich — Wydział Ewidencji i Statystyki

Karta rejestracyjna Nr *8170/st*

2612

1. Nazwisko *Przepiórka*
   (dla mężatek panieńskie)
2. Imiona *Fricia*
   (używane podkreślić)
3. Urodzony(a) dn. *14* mies. ___ roku *1939*
   w *Hajrow*
4. Rodzice *Mendel i Elena*
   (imię ojca, imię i nazwisko panieńskie matki)
5. Adres z 1 IX.39 *Hajrow*
6. Zmiany adresu w czasie wojny

DATA	ADRES	PRZYCZYNA ZMIANY
40-4)		

7. Adres obecny *Wwa Busme 19*

8. Wykształcenie

9. Zawód
   a) wyuczony ___ gdzie
   b) wykonywany przed wojną
   c) wykonywany w czasie wojny

   d) obecny
   Sposób przetrwania *Harno Org/an*

יוסף, בן ר' פנחס זרבל פשפיורקה, אשתי מלכה (לבית
דרהוביצקי). ילדיהם: היה, יעקב, שרה, נחז בניהם
שבסביבת רוובניצה, החזיקו מעמד עד סוף המלחמה, 1944,
ונורו ע"י הנאצים ביער.

מנדל פשפיורקה, בן ר' פנחס זרבל' היה חבר פרדיצ
סמאל, חבר מועצת העיר. נוספה באקציה השניה בטרבלינקה
ב-1943. אשתי אסתר (לבית פניובסקי) וילדיהם זיליק,
יצהק, ניסלה (ניצלה בעזרת נוצרים וחיה באה"ב).

Laws forbidding Poles to give any aid to Jews in original German

BEKANNTMACHUNG

Betrifft.
Beherbergung von geflüchteten Juden

Es besteht Anlass zu folgendem Hinweis:
Gemäss der 3. Verordnung über Aufenthalts-
beschränkungen im Generalgouvernement
vom 15.10.1941 (VO Bl. GG S. 595) unterliegen
Juden, die den jüdischen Wohnbezirk unbe-
fugt verlassen, der Todesstrafe.

Gemäss der gleichen Vorschrift unterliegen Perso-
nen, die solchen Juden wissentlich Unterschlupf gewähren
usw. Nahrung verabfolgen oder verkaufen, ebenfalls
in gleichfalls der Todesstrafe.

Die nichtjüdische Bevölkerung wird da-
her dringend gewarnt:

1) Juden Unterschlupf zu gewähren,
2) Juden Beköstigung zu verabfolgen,
3) Juden Nahrungsmittel zu verkaufen.

Tschenstochau den 24. 9. 42

OGŁOSZENIE

Dotyczy.
przetrzymywania ukrywających się Żydów.

Zachodzi potrzeba przypomnienia, że sto-
sownie do § 3 Rozporządzenia o ograniczeniach
pobytu w Gen. Gub. z dnia 15. X. 1941 roku
(Dz. Rozp. dla GG. str. 595) Żydzi, opuszczający
dzielnicę żydowską bez zezwolenia, podlegają
karze śmierci.

Według tego rozporządzenia osoby, które tym
Żydom świadomie udzielają schronienia, dostarczają im
pożywienia, lub sprzedają artykuły żywnościowe — gra-
również karze śmierci.

Niniejszem ostrzega się stanowczo ludność
nieżydowską przed:

1) udzielaniem Żydom przytułku,
2) dostarczaniem im jedzenia,
3) sprzedawaniem im artykułów
żywnościowych.

Częstochowa, dnia 24. 9. 42

Der Stadthauptmann
Dr. Franke

CITATIONS PART 1—POLAND

1. http://kehilalinks.iewishgen.org/Wegrow/history.html Kehilat Wengrow: Sefer Zikaron, "Introduction"
2. Beit Hatfutzot, information flyer, Tel Aviv, Israel
3. **From a Ruined Garden pp.91-94.) #4 Kugelmass put in body #4 Kugelmass et al
4. http://kehilalinks.iewishgen.0rg/Wegrow/svnagogue.html
5. Bielawsky, Shraga Feivel, Louis W. Liebovich, ed. The Last Jew from Wegrow: *The Memoirs of a Survivor of the Step-by-Step Genocide in Poland.* Praeger, NY. C 1991 by Shraga Feivel Bielawsky & Louis W. Liebovich
6. Kugelmas, From a Ruined Garden pp. 91-94.)
7. https://kehilalinks.jewishgen.org/Wegrow/vengrov-pre-war.html (Map)
8. http://kehilalinks.jewishgen.org/Wegrow/history.html market square
9. http://kehilalinks.iewishgenorg/Wegrow/svnagogue.html
10. https://kehilalinks.iewishgen.org/Wegrow/bola.html Pictures of beautiful children. ltka and Bola Przepiorka (2) Fishel Przepiorka
11. https://www.geni.com/proiects/Alexander-Rabbinical-Dynastv/68 Alexander Chasidic movement
12. https://kehilalinks.iewishgen.org/Wegrow/ptak-4.html Polish schools
13. Bielawsky, op.cit.
14. *Kehilat Wegrow, Sefer Zikaron, (written in Hebrew and Yiddish) Tamari*, M. editor, former residents of Wegrow in Israel, Tel Aviv, Israel, 1961.
15. Bielawsky, op cit.

16. *https://en.wikipedia.org/wiki/Timeline_of_Treblinka_extermination_camp*
17. *Bielawsky, op.cit*
18. *International Red Cross, My father's death certificate*
19. Sefer Zikaron p. 380, Norma, Chaya, Perl and Feige
20. https://en.wikipedia.org/wiki/History_of_the_Jews_in_20th-century_Poland Decrees about helping Jews, p. 20.
21. https://blogs.transparent.com/polish/do-you-know-most-of-the-prayers-in-polish/ Prayer to Mary in Polish and English
22. https://www.holocausthistoricalsociety.org.uk/contents/ghettoss-z/wegrow.html statistics of survivors
23. https://www.google.com/search?q=children%27s+home+in+otwock+poland&tbm=isch&tbs=rimg:CZwUwFYHPgA-CljjAe6Y5Siux73smeMltkxEn7wk8vTdmPNLQPkaqeJz3Ed-Fq0S3ECh18b0eRa6ynREGdkfgA5MSBbyoSCcB7pjlKK7HvEQxobPRtO5ejKhlJeyZ4wi2TEScR8QupQAwlFvlqEgnvCTy9N2Y80hFEcYku53DnOyoSCdA-Rqp4nPcREb2X-LrwCrtAZKhIJ0WrRLcQKHXwRQlibk-na1ulqEglvR5Frr-KdEQRFEcYku53DnOvoSCZ0p-ADkxlFvEURxiS7ncOc7&tbo=u&sa=X&ved=0ahUKEwiUqpG97YTXAhXL5YMKHeW0A8oQ9C8lhw&biw=1080&bih=572&dpr=1#imgrc=nBTAVgc-AAJafM Me at Otwock,
24. HTTP://WWW.YADVASHEM.ORG/YV/EN/EXHIBITIONS/OTWOCK/HOME.ASP about services and support of Dom Dziecka building
25. Jewish Historical Institute, Anna P. Drozd
26. Canadian Jewish Congress file, Adara Goldberg
27. **Hillel, in Pirkei Avot 2:5: (The Wisdom of the Fathers, tractate of the Mishnah, Part of the Talmud
28. Bielawski, op cit. p. 94
29. The Book of Ruth 1:16 (negation of Ruth's speech to Naomi)

PART 2

❧

SWEDEN, A STRANGER ONCE MORE

CHAPTER 1

LIFE IN AN ORPHANAGE

It was January 1947. I was eight years old. I wasn't told where I was going or to which country I was going. Before I got to the Swedish Orphanage that I do remember, I had to stay at a children's home called Fiskeby-Vardhem, near Stockholm, run by the JDC (Joint Distribution Committee) and UNRRA. These two organizations opened field offices in the American Zone after the war. Orphaned children became a top priority there for these children were to get rest, food, clothing, and medical attention. I was examined, even given a Wasserman test, and found to be in excellent health. (Citation #1, Canadian War Orphans file)

There are other kernels of memory here. I remember visiting a Jewish family and meeting a teenage girl named Rachel. How long did I stay there? Possibly more than overnight. Two facts are indelible in my memory: Jewish and oranges. A point was made that this family was Jewish, and Rachel was so happy they could finally get oranges. I had never tasted an orange. "Smell it," she said, and then asked, "Do you want to taste it?" I didn't but was repeatedly encouraged to do so. I wasn't ecstatic about the taste of those oranges. They certainly were not as delicious as the cherries in that distant, long ago garden. But otherwise, I remember very few details of this time period. I must assume I was traumatized after abruptly leaving *Matka*.

Soon thereafter, I recollect seeing a huge building. I spotted ladies with long habits and white headgear. (Later, I learned they were Lutheran Nuns). Everyone looked the same. How would I learn who was who? I had to answer to a new name now. No longer was I Gucia, but the Swedish equivalent, Guta. I was no longer Kowalczyk, but Przepiorka again. I had to familiarize myself with my old-new last name.

There was a large room with bins of clothes. The clothes were arranged by size, and separately for boys and girls. I remember picking clothes from another bin of clothing, at Dom Dziecka in Otwock, and was puzzled as to why I had to pick clothes again. I had my own room and was responsible for keeping it neat and clean. If I did that poorly, there were consequences. I don't remember what they were, but they left me with a habit of neatness. I continued folding my clothes when I came to my next stop and even in my own home now.

At meal time, we ate at six-feet oblong tables, no cozy kitchen table, no vat of fresh milk from the cow. Almost every meal included herring! I hated herring! I would throw it under the table trying to reach a few places beyond my own chair. Soon the kids noticed how much I hated it and began bullying me. One would hold me, and another tried to force herring down my throat. I gagged or threw up. I also had strabismus, crossed eyes, a perfect target for teasing. There were so many children at the orphanage, but I had no friends or even playmates.

There was, however, one little boy, probably a year or two younger than I was, who smiled a lot at me and followed me around. Very early on, I smiled at him and said hello. He didn't respond. When I was learning to ride a bike! And the counselor finally let me go, I yelled to him, "Look at me! I'm learning to ride a bike! Do you want learn, too?" No reaction. Something seemed wrong. I couldn't talk to him and he wouldn't talk to me. I found out he was both deaf and mute. I wonder to this day what hell he had experienced. Did he see his mother killed in front of his eyes? Did he see his baby sister thrown into a pit and shot? Was the shooting around him, aimed at him, so loud that he had to escape the raucous, deadly noise and refuse to hear? Was he smiling because I was smiling at him, finally a human gesture in his life? Was he smiling because he was standing on his own two feet in a quiet, peaceful setting? Or was he just grateful to be alive?

Gucia (now Guta) in Sweden learning to ride a bike.
The little boy was my deaf and mute friend.

I eventually did learn to ride a bike. The photograph shows it was an adult-size bike, without training wheels. Very soon after the older girl, probably a counselor, let go of the bike, off I went!

Shortly after that, I was experiencing throat pain. I had the painful surgery to have my tonsils removed. The vanilla ice cream afterwards tasted delicious!

Within a short time, maybe two or three months, I was no longer speaking Polish. I had a new vocabulary, and I was speaking Swedish! I don't remember having a difficult time communicating. Somehow, I was understood, and comprehended what was being said. Now I could speak two languages: Polish and Swedish! My time here was a period of personal growth, and I may have gained a clearer understanding of my past.

(Document listing orphans coming to Sweden from Poland) I don't know my exact date of arrival, but I probably stayed in the orphanage from April 1947 to December 12, 1947, just under a year. So I experienced almost a full seasonal cycle, the warmth of spring through mountains of snow in winter. I especially loved the unusual sled on skis. I sat in a chair above ground, and someone held on to handles on the back of the chair, with her feet on what looked like skis, the skis the chair was on. I loved that!

https://commons.wikimedia.org/w/index.php?curid=3607035 #2 citation

Though disorienting, life was expanding for me here. I was exposed to another culture, and another religion, Protestantism, though I didn't know the difference between that and Catholicism. But somehow, I felt it was different from being Jewish. Many people were responsible for me, but there was no one in a meaningful relationship with me. I missed *Matka's* hugs.

I do, however, recall a pleasant time around Christmas. I witnessed an unusual sight. I saw a woman with a crown of lit candles on her head! I was awed! This was so beautiful! Around Christmas time in Sweden, one of the biggest celebrations is St. Lucia's Day (or St. Lucy's Day) on December 13th. St. Lucia's Day is now celebrated by a girl dressing in a white dress with a red sash round her waist and a crown of candles on her head. Small children use electric candles but after the age of twelve, real candles are used. The young woman in the orphanage allowed me to walk with her as the candles glowed. But I was never allowed a crown of candles. I only remembered a crown of flowers made by *Matka*.

Unlike my previous departure, here I had no great attachment or love and loss to overcome. I had no difficulty leaving this nest. However, a short time after I came to my next stop, Montreal, Canada, I was moved to write a thank you note to King Gustav V. He never answered me.

Reflecting upon this time in my life, I am stunned by the number of documents and dates that punctuate it. There are no significant personal relationships to enrich me. Documents show I was in Warsaw in January of 1947 leaving for Sweden, and then leaving for Montreal on December 12, 1947.

I spent years trying to ascertain how I got to Sweden and then to Canada with such long intervals in between before being allowed to enter the USA. Who got me from the airport in Warsaw to the orphanage? Who was the woman with the scratches on her face? Why did I have to stay at the Swedish orphanage for almost a year? Who was responsible for getting me from one continent to another? Why did I have to stay in Canada for over three years when it was only supposed to be for three weeks?

Quite unbelievably, this mystery was solved with the help of a questionnaire from a PhD researcher from Canada. I was notified that a post-doctoral fellow, Adara Goldberg of Stockton University, was doing research on Holocaust survivor war orphans adopted by Canadian families. I immediately contacted her and gave her my early background. Indeed, I qualified and agreed to answer some of her questions. One of them was totally puzzling to me: "When did your American relatives arrange for your participation in the War Orphans Project?" The War Orphans Project, I had never heard of it. So before I received the information from her, I immediately turned to the Encyclopedia Britannica of 2017 Google. http://www.virtualmuseum.ca/sgc-cms/expositions-exhibitions/orphelins-orphans/enelish/themes/where/paee2.html #3 Sure enough, the description of that program seemed to fit with my scant knowledge of my journey. The documents and memories seemed to match this program's requirements:

1. "In 1947 the Canadian government issued the Order in Council #1647 granting permission for 1000 Jewish war orphans to enter Canada." I came in 1947 and was an orphan.

2. "The Congress and the UNRRA worked to find orphans under the age of eighteen." I saw those UNRRA armbands before boarding a ship. I was eight years old.

3. Some waited in orphanages or DP camps for years before they could come. I waited almost a whole year in an orphanage.

4. To qualify, they were screened, observed, and given medical examinations. "To be granted a visa they had to express their desire to come to Canada and demonstrate "the ability to adjust." Sometimes immigration officials excluded children who wore glasses or could not read." That's me—at eight with an interrupted education, could I read in a foreign language or express my desire to come to Canada? I also wore glasses. Maybe that's why it took so long?

5. "Most entered the country through Halifax." I did.

6. Of the 1123 young survivors finally admitted, only thirty-seven were under ten years of age. That could explain why on one of the pages of the ship's manifest, I am the only eight-year-old among the adolescent children listed. We all arrived in Canada December 20, 1947. (Facts checked on this page: of the total, 70% were boys, but on this page more of them were girls)

7. "At first the young survivors 'demonstrated unusual behaviors'." I did. I mention them in the Montreal segment of the book.

8. "These orphans displayed resilience and the ability to adjust…they learned English quickly." I did and described it in the Montreal section.

9. I was part of the War Orphans Project. This knowledge has clarified many puzzling questions. Perhaps there will be additional puzzles solved.

I found myself going through a long line of children, actually at a London airport to eventually take the Aquitania ship, and being handed chicklets by people wearing UNRRA armbands.

They smiled as they gave out individual packets of chicklets. I didn't know what these little white squares were. My first foray into chewing gum!

I realized there was another strange woman taking care of me. Was she an UNRRA representative?

Date	6.4.49		
Name	PRZEPIORKA, Gucia		File F 18-108
BD 1939	BP		Nat Polish-Jew.
Next of Kin	parents: Mendel & Estera		Book P. p. 160
Source of Information	Centr. Jew. Committee in Poland, Warsaw		
Last kn. Location	Warszawa, Brzeska 19		Date aft. war Jan. 4.
CC/Prison		Arr.	lib.
Transf. on		to	
Died on		in	
Cause of death			
Buried on		in	
Grave			D. C. No.
Remarks	address in 1939 : Magra Wegrow		

"The United Nations Relief and Rehabilitation Administration (UNRRA) was created at a 44-nation conference at the White House on November 9, 1943. Its mission was to provide economic assistance to European nations after World War II and to repatriate and assist the refugees who would come under Allied control. The U.S. government funded close to half of UNRRA's budget."
https://www.ushmm.orq/wlc/en/article.
php?Moduleld=10005685 Citation #

CHAPTER 2

ABOUT SWEDEN

Sweden granted citizenship to Jews in 1870. (Citation #4 HC p.28). It also had a tradition of non-participation in European conflicts. Hence, it maintains its reputation as neutral.

A Polish jurist, Raphael Lemkin, did his work on crimes and persecution, which led to his coining the word genocide while living in Sweden. Ironically, Sweden did not participate in the genocide, but its economy benefitted from Germany's war effort. Still, as Germany's brutality became more severe, Sweden accepted almost the entire Jewish population of Denmark and took Jewish children in after the Holocaust (Holoc. Chron. P. 572, Citation #5).

The extent of Sweden's neutrality is debated, and its relationship with Jews and policy toward Jews is highly nuanced. The specific years of the Nazi period and the relationship of Germany and the Soviet Union with Sweden's Scandinavian neighbors Norway and Finland also influenced the actions Sweden took toward Jews. Economic considerations fueled certain behaviors of Sweden as well. The Germans considered Swedes almost as Aryan as themselves, just as they considered Denmark its Aryan cousin and allowed most of the Danish Jewish population to be sent there.

Sweden provided Germany with many machine parts for its war industry and helped move German troops and war equipment through Sweden from Norway to the Eastern front in Finland. Trade with Germany helped the Swedish economy.

Sweden was part of Germany's cultural sphere. Martin Luther was German. In addition, there were Swedish Nazis and Anti-Semitism had existed in Sweden, albeit at certain periods more than others.

There were four distinct periods of Swedish-Jewish involvement:

1. From 1933 to 1938: What happened to Jews didn't affect Sweden and its interests.
2. From 1938 to 1939: The "Jewish Problem" gained importance, especially since there were now Jewish refugees from Austria and Czechoslovakia after Hitler marched into these countries in 1938.
3. From 1939 to 1942: Sweden was very concerned about the violence against Jews, but at the same time struggled to avoid participating in the war and avoid foreign entanglements as it historically intended.
4. From 1942 to 1945: Sweden actively responded to help Jews. Sweden allowed children to go there from German-occupied countries during the war. Sweden also orchestrated the rescue of the Danes by ferrying Jews from Denmark into Sweden on fishing boats thereby saving almost the entire Jewish population of Denmark.

The above from: The Stones Cry Out p.45, 46 give citation # 6

Beyond intervals of humanitarian involvement and neutrality, Sweden can claim some outstanding heroes. For instance:

> A group of Swedes headed by Sven Norman, head of a Swedish engineering company ASEA, in Warsaw, Poland, was instrumental in notifying the world about the atrocities that were being perpetrated on Jews in Warsaw in 1942. Because of his position, Norman was able to

enter the ghetto, take thousands of pictures including such details as showing Jews not being allowed on the sidewalk if there was a German passing by. He and several of his Swedish expatriates working form other corporations, (later to become Swedish Match and mobile phone giant, Ericsson) were able to help the *Armia Krajowa* (The Polish Home Army) by smuggling in documents and money and communicating with the Polish Government in exile in London. They were eventually caught but were saved by the intervention of King Gustav (Hitler admired royalty) and Germany's need for Sweden's supply of iron and ball bearings for its weapons. Sven Norman was honored by the *Armia Krajowa* for telling the world about the Holocaust. When interviewed in the 1970s and asked why he risked his life, Norman replied: "During my entire life, I was a businessman. I liked my job and I was good in my field. I joined the struggle because I wanted to do something that was not for profit for once in my life." (The above from "Martyrdom & Resistance" Jan/Feb 2015, p.5.) Citation #7

How differently things might have occurred if others had had similar thoughts.

Chronology:

- Sept. 19, 1946 - A special emissary is awaiting me in Sweden
- Oct. 15, 1946 - Application for my passport is made
- Oct. 21, 1946, Mrs. Allberg receives my Passport to go to Sweden

- Nov. 1946 I leave Dom Dziecka for Sweden (Note" ***2. Purchasing power of the cost of my trip from Sweden to Canada, $380 in 1947. In 2017 that cost is $4,257.17!!! https://www.moneysavingtips.org/calculate/inflation/380 - THIS SHOWS THE GENEROSITY AND WEALTH OF my Aunt Esther and Uncle Max Bernstein at that time)
- Nov. 1946 to Ian. '47 - Canadian documents indicate that I remember staying with my Aunt and then an orphanage in Poland. It was possible that I stayed at Foehrenwald with Aunt Norma for a few weeks-(as per The Canadian War Orphans Project) I remember being there, but probably life there was not extraordinary in any way, and I was safe with an aunt, so I don't remember any activities other than seeing her serve her chicken soup. I do have a vague memory that I also helped her serve the chicken soup to some survivors there.
- Jan. '47 to April '47, I went to the Mosaiska Forsamlingen home, run by the JDC (Joint

Distribution Committee) and UNRRA.

April '47 to Dec. '47 I was transferred to Fiskeby-Vardhem, the Lutheran Orphanage in

Sweden. I remember this place a bit better.

The above information is from the translated documents of The Jewish Historical Institute, (Anna Przybyszewska Drozd) and a file from the Canadian Jewish Congress Archives (Adara Goldberg) Citation #1

Copy of Doc. No. 87425464 #1 (3.3.2.1/01/105/0026)
In conformity with the ITS Archives list

Swedish document showing my arrival in Sweden in 1947 and my departure in 1947. And another document shows I left Warsaw to Sweden in January 1947, so my entire stay at two Swedish orphanages was almost a whole year.

Copy of Doc. No. 78779183 #1 (3.1.1.3/0001-0197/0040/0125)
In conformity with the ITS Archives emigration

Ship document showing my name, Przepiorka, Gucia, as one of
the youngest orphans going to Canada in 1947

This little "Przepiorka" did not sing very much in this cold nest.
Perhaps the next one would be warmer.

CITATIONS PART 2—SWEDEN

1. Canadian Jewish Congress Archives (Adara Goldberg) War Orphans File (My medical examination) Also from Jewish Historical Institute, Anna Przybyszewska Drozd translation.
2. https://commons.wikimedia.org/w/index.php?curid=3607035 ski - chair picture
3. http://www.virtualmuseum.ca/sgc-cms/expositions-exhibitions/orphelins-orphans/english/themes/where/page2.html war orphans project description
4. Holocaust Chronicle, p. 28 (Sweden granting citizenship to Jews)
5. Holocaust Chronicle, P. 572) (Sweden saves Danish Jews)
6. Koblik, Steven. The Stones Cry Out: Sweden's Response to the Persecution of the Jews 1939-1945. Holocaust Library, NY. 1988 *p.45, 46,* (Swedish Jewish involvement)
7. "Martyrdom & Resistance" Jan/Feb 2015, p.5.) Citation #6)

PART 3

&

MONTREAL

CHAPTER 1

ARRIVAL AND NEW BEGINNINGS

My life is a series of arrivals and departures; tracing and untying knots, unions, and separations; of unfolding, withdrawing, planning; finding, reaching, attaining, gaining and losing. Thrust like a seed in a random breeze, I arrived in Montreal December 20, 1947, having left Sweden on December 12, 1947. The Aquitania, a ship under British registry, arrived in Halifax, Nova Scotia with its precious cargo: orphans. Recent information on the Canadian War Orphans Project has filled in this gap in my background; I was part of this Canadian rescue operation. I've also learned from the ship's passenger list that I was one of the youngest of the orphans on the ship. Only my birth year is listed, and the list includes many teenage boys who made up the majority of the total number of orphans. Incidentally, my name is misspelled on the passenger list; I am included as Przepiorka Gucia, and then Przepiorka, Gloria, age eight.

I was seasick for the entire eight-day trip. I had the top bunk bed on the ship. I kept putting my head over the railing on the top deck to throw up. A young woman, Fela, (whose last name I don't know), was in charge of me. Perhaps she was one of the UNRRA assistants. Older teens and young adults were in charge of younger ones. As mentioned earlier, I was part of the War Orphans Project sponsored by the Canadian Jewish Congress in conjunction with UNRRA (United Nations Relief and Rehabilitation Administration,

1943 to 1946). Among the thirty-seven children under age ten was this dark, curly-haired, cross-eyed, eight-year-old little girl with her cardboard suitcase in which she carried some ill-fitting clothing and her most precious possession, a framed picture of Jesus. *Matka* considered Jesus a grounding and unchanging source of security for me. I am sure she felt Jesus would protect me.

Where was I going to live now? Would I have friends? Would I grow to love anyone? Would anyone love me? Could I remain with them if I wanted to? I was to learn the answers to these questions as the blurry future became the present in Montreal.

A few hours after leaving Halifax, the train arrives in Montreal. Montreal's Windsor train station is crowded.

I am walking in another strange place. I am frightened, alone, surrounded by the unfamiliar, the unknown, and the unfathomable. A cacophony of strange sounds and lights at the arrival platform from Halifax creates a frantic scene. Suddenly, I hear a voice: "There she is! There's my brother's little girl!" This is my aunt, Esther Bernstein, in a fashionable winter-white hat, wearing bottle green ankle-strap shoes to match her smart-looking suit. I don't know how she knew who I was. She must have seen pictures of me to be able to identify me. A short, chubby woman with beautiful ankles, she is my father's oldest sister who had immigrated to America before WWII. She is waiting with members of the Morantz and Rothstein family, about ten people who are strangers to me, and most of them, even to her.

Fannie (nee Rothstein) and Abie Morantz, both from Eastern Europe, and my Aunt Esther and Uncle Max are not old friends. They met once at a wedding in New York. Aunt Esther made a request: "I have a little girl coming from Poland, my brother's only living child. She needs to be in Canada for about three weeks 'til her immigration number comes up. The lawyer needs about three weeks to complete the paperwork. Then she will be allowed to immigrate to New York. Can you take her for those weeks? I'll pay all the expenses." The Morantzs agreed without hesitation. These facts were confirmed recently in a telephone conversation with Shirley and Rita, daughters of Fannie and Abie. Rita, then sixteen, was actually at that wedding and remembers Esther making that request. And Shirley remembers her mother telling the family they will have a little girl living with them for a few weeks. "We were all anxious to see this little immigrant, and were happy about it," she added.

I got a gold locket with two little diamonds from Esther and Max when I arrived in Canada. I still have it, though I removed the diamonds and reused them elsewhere. The inscription on the back— "from Max and Esther to Gitele"—seems to me, today, to be so cold and impersonal in comparison to what I would like the message to *have* said. I would have preferred "dear", "love" and "welcome" somewhere in there. But at age eight, when I got this beautiful piece of jewelry, the likes of which I had never seen before, I was excited.

My new nest, the Morantz home, was a walk-up apartment on the second floor at 22 Fairmount West in Montreal. It consisted of a small foyer with an eat-in kitchen and spacious dining room on the left, the large master bedroom straight ahead, and a living room and a smaller bedroom on the right. The master bedroom, where I would sleep the night I arrived, had a double bed, two dressers, and a single bed in the corner on the left side of the door. None of the clothes I had brought with me matched or even fit properly. But I folded them neatly before going to bed every night as I had been taught in the Swedish orphanage where our rooms were checked for neatness daily. I found a new, white chintz robe with red roses on it on my bed. I folded that neatly on the chair, too. Here I was to begin my search for childhood. A normal childhood.

The Morantz household consisted of Fannie and Abie, the parents, daughter Rita (around eighteen), and son Stanley (fifteen years). The older daughter, Shirley, was already married and living with her husband, Jack, in their own apartment on Maplewood Avenue, a streetcar ride away. I could not understand anyone's English conversations, only their facial expressions. Fannie and Abie were not newcomers to Canada. They actually got married in Montreal, at the

Fairmount Shul (synagogue) in 1924. But Fannie was still fluent in Polish, my mother tongue, so I could speak to her in Polish. Since I was hearing English all around me, I understood it perfectly within three months, and could even speak it. But I refused. It was easier to speak Polish; Polish was familiar and comfortably easy.

Fanny was a consummate homemaker. The aromas in her kitchen wafted through the apartment. She made scrumptious roast chicken, moist on the inside but with crispy skin and potato kugel that I have tried since to replicate but can't; flavorful, rich chicken soup; sometimes brisket which was brought home by Abie from the meat market where he worked. I kept referring to chicken by its Polish word *kurka*, and even taught Rita this word. I could eat *kurka* three times a day! This was Abie's lunch after *shul* on Saturday. The house was crowded, but never messy. In the morning, the sweet aroma of hot cocoa permeated the house. Fannie's blueberry buns were legendary. I remember her future son-in-law, Buzzy, looking in the pantry in Val Morin, our summer home in the Laurentian Mountains a few hours from Montreal. He saw cookie sheets of blueberry buns neatly arranged. He was afraid to take one, thinking Fannie was a caterer and these were counted out for a specific order.

Abie was a portly man and often walked with his hands behind him. He wore a hat, a beautifully tailored suit, white shirt, and tie; he was always elegant for synagogue on the holidays and for special occasions. He held his head up and looked proud. His three children, though now adults, called him Daddy and referred to him that way when talking to each other. Shirley and Rita always made sure he had a nice new suit for *Rosh Hashanah* or for a wedding or bar mitzvah.

I never heard him raise his voice. I had seen him angry or upset with Fannie, but always in an almost silent way, with a contorted facial expression. During the week, he worked for Morantz Beef, the *Bonsecours* meat market owned by one of his relatives. He left early in the morning and came home late. When I first arrived in Montreal, I did not understand who he was. I thought he was a boarder. He turned out to be the gentlest, kindest father I ever knew. But I still needed to *feel* safe and secure. I cautioned everyone in the house to "hide the knives," remembering how Michal held the knife to *Matka's* throat. In addition, whenever someone I didn't know came to the house, man or woman, I hid under the bed. Perhaps the memory of the soldiers scaring me in the middle of the night or having to live underground resurfaced. After I stopped hiding, I would latch on to Fannie's apron or dress when I didn't know that person, and avert my eyes, sometimes my whole face. Painfully shy, I didn't say hello or engage in any conversation.

Rita was blonde, blue eyed, always perfectly coiffed and fashionably dressed, and had a model's figure. I was amazed, even after I left Montreal and returned for visits, how many different ways she could wear her hair! Almost monthly, she had a new hairstyle. And looked terrific in each of them! She had a magenta coat with a high collar which highlighted her fair, clear skin. Beautiful does not even come close to describing her!

She worked for a man named Mendl. She may have mentioned that name once or twice, but I still remember her boss's name, perhaps because that was also my father's name. Her other duty was to walk me to school in the morning and get me home at lunchtime, even though it meant she couldn't enjoy lunch with her friends and co-workers. As an eight-year-old, I was not allowed to cross the busy and dangerous St. Urban Street by myself. I recall her in a letter on her seventy-fifth birthday.

Looking back Eishet Chayil seventy-fifth birthday:

*Eishet Chayil, A Woman of Valor
(by Gloria Glantz)

*Woman of Valor, or Eishet Chayil in Hebrew,
is a hymn that rounds out the book of Proverbs.
The poem speaks of a woman of valor as one who is
strong and righteous. I adapted it for Rita.*

Citation # 1
As a woman of valor

Who can qualify?
She who is treasured by those who know her.
She extends her helping hands
And her humane heart
Even when her own heart is heavy and in pain.
Her generosity and strength
Are quietly extraordinary.
She befriends, comforts, consoles, and brings joy.
Each day of her life is graced by her gentleness
of spirit.
She is unique, and her beauty is all encompassing.
She is
My sister, Rita

Even after the tragic, untimely death of their son, Dougie, for whom I babysat on a New Year's Eve when I was eleven, Rita and Buzzy attended our daughter Jordana's wedding on May 28, 2000. They came with heavy hearts but heartfelt warm wishes for us.

Stanley, the Morantz's only son, was a handsome boy with a noticeably crooked nose. He accepted me, though sometimes good naturedly teased me. He was somewhat rebellious. I remember his having a very painful ear infection and having to put ear drops in his ears. He absolutely refused to get those drops in his ears, slamming the door as he ran out of the apartment, down the stairs, screaming. "No! No! No!" Other times I was his banker, lending him some spending money from my 25-cent allowance which I was saving to buy a Cadbury chocolate bar once a week.

The first several months after my arrival, I was still called by my Polish name, Gucia. Actually, Rita's fiancé, Buzzy, and his friends all called me Gooch. They were affectionately teasing me. But it was so frequent, I became annoyed. I sulked and scowled. If he didn't want me to understand something, Buzzy would use pig-Latin. This is a form of a made-up language where one removes the first letter of a word, puts it at the end of the word, and ads "ay" at the end. So for example, the word sick would sound "icksnay". Eventually I became proficient in understanding this new pseudo-language.

One day, my new adopted sister Shirley declared, "Gucia, Guta, what kinds of names are these? Your name is Gloria!" My second name also changed. Because I was living with the Morantz family, I was now Gloria Morantz. Name number four in eight years of living.

Already several months had passed, and the estimated three weeks with the Morantz family grew to sixteen weeks. My life with *Matka* and even with orphans in Sweden began to recede into a fading history. I was starting a new adventure being a Morantz family member. Passover was coming. That's when I got an order from Rita, "Pesach is coming. No Polish allowed in this house." She was emphatic. She looked right into my eyes. "You have to start speaking English, or at least Yiddish, but not Polish!"

Yiddish? I was permitted to speak Yiddish? Anything Yiddish was forbidden to me from age three to six at *Matka's*. Now I was actually learning Yiddish in school! What a liberating feeling!

As befits a normal childhood, education was a central aspect of life. There were two schools on Fairmount Street, right next to each other. One was the Fairmount School, a public school, free and reputed to have some rough kids. The other was the Jewish People's School referred to as JPS (Yiddishe Folk Shule), founded 1914. This one charged a tuition fee. The principal was Mr. Wiseman and the assistant principal was Mr. Zigman. It was decided I would go to JPS. There I would be with Jewish children and learn Hebrew and Yiddish besides the regular curriculum of arithmetic, reading, geography, and French.

I was eight years old and placed into first grade. I hardly understood my Jewish classmates.

Some would tease me about my crossed eyes. "Cockeyed Jennie! Where'd your eye go?" I walked with my head down, hiding my eyes. I was shy and uncommunicative.

Hebrew and Yiddish subjects were easier for me. I was very excited when my sixth grade Hebrew teacher, Mr. Wilchesky, appeared in the choir at the Fairmount Shul (synagogue)! I loved his voice, even his speaking voice. Do eleven- or twelve-year-olds even notice a teacher's voice unless it's particularly grating or unpleasant? Did my awareness of this hearken back to the appreciation of my mother's beautiful voice and my love of music? Or to Jack Ginsberg, Shirley's husband, who also gave me his beautiful voice and love of opera? Mr. Wilchesky's height forced him to bend his head down when he walked through a doorway, so I could pick him out in the choir easily. Seeing my teacher in the choir was a draw for me to go to synagogue.

My fifth grade Hebrew teacher, Mr. Chaitman, wrote on my report card that I was a good student. In his class, I was picked to be Vashti in a Purim play. I didn't like that; I wanted to be the beautiful Queen Esther! I think Vashti was a larger part and Mr. Chaitman assumed I'd have no trouble memorizing it. I had no acting ability, but I could memorize lines easily.

I was always conscientious about doing my schoolwork and homework. Perhaps this trait was connected to my future desire to be a teacher. Why did I strive toward that goal? Was it because I liked school, my friends, and my kind teachers? I don't think that as an eleven-year-old, I considered that it was a socially accepted profession for women.

If I wasn't sure about the homework or an assignment was unclear, I would yell to Fannie: *Zazvontche Zigmana!* (Call Mr. Zigman). My understanding teachers noticed I was having problems with reading, geography, and arithmetic. I got an F in Arithmetic on the first and second report card and only a G ("Good") in Geography, and comments on the back of the card: "Gloria, you have two subjects that need hard work—Geography and Arithmetic. Please come to us for all the help you need," wrote Miss Friedman and Miss Yellin. That was in fifth grade. In spite of the kindness of my teachers, I still had to bear the unkind teasing by some classmates about my crossed eyes.

Eventually, when I came to understand and speak English, the teasing subsided, and I began to love school! It was a new and familiar experience. That may sound contradictory. But I loved learning new things and I loved having a routine, knowing what was happening each day. I felt more secure that I wasn't going to be thrown into a new, uncontrollable situation. I didn't want to miss school on any day.

Outside of school, numerous relatives came to visit Fannie and Abie frequently. The Morantz's extended family members were numerous and blessed with longevity. The relatives came to visit Fannie and Abie frequently, especially when I first arrived, to see the little Polish refugee girl who had landed on their doorstep. They always arrived bearing gifts for little Gucia. Auntie Yettie and Uncle Philip brought a red plastic tea set. It included little red cups and saucers, a miniature teapot, creamer, and sugar bowl. When company came over, I displayed the tea set. "Tea with sugar, with milk, or both? Would anyone like lemon?" I was not just pretending to be a hostess, but also became a very young entrepreneur. I was charging a penny per cup! And they bought!

Another toy I got was a little crib and a doll that could open and close her eyes! A little reminder of a previous doll? I put her into her crib each night and covered her with a small towel blanket. I slept in a folding single bed in the dining room. The bed was comfortable enough and I never minded having to open and close it. But for about a year after I arrived, I was always being chased, running away, hiding from someone in my dream-filled sleep. I had a fear of being caught. Often, I was so grateful to wake up so I could stop running away and worrying about being caught. Was this a dormant memory of being caught at *Matka's* by not performing like a good Christian? Could I be caught telling some untruth which would reveal I was Jewish? This fear had followed me across to another continent.

The little crib was right near me. When the bed was folded in the morning, the little crib had its own space by the wall near the bed, waiting for the next night. Perhaps this safe space with my little crib contributed to my eventual more peaceful, restful sleep. I was almost nine years old, playing with tea sets, dolls, and cribs.

The Morantz always made sure someone was with me if they had to be out. One late afternoon on a weekend, Fannie and Able had to go out, Stanley wasn't home, and Rita was also out. Who was going to stay with me? They had no babysitter. Fannie provided a solution. "Gloria, we'll pay you. You can be your own babysitter." I agreed. I was losing my fearfulness. Even then I knew the value of a buck!

The Morantz family certainly knew the value of money. I had to turn off the lights when I left a room. Any room in the apartment that was not in use was not to have the lights turned on. The radio, the only source of news and entertainment, also had to be turned off if there was no one physically in the room. I still do that. I learned to be frugal in other ways. When Rita was getting married, out-of-town guests were expected. Fannie wanted to ascertain if they would be coming to the wedding if they hadn't sent back the response card yet. So they made a phone call. At that time, if you wanted to talk to a specific person, it was a "person to person" call and was more expensive. You could hear the voice on the other end pick up, you could recognize the voice, and a cryptic message would come through. Who's this? It's Mrs. Cummings. Well, you didn't want to talk to Mrs. Cummings. There was no Mrs. Cummings! But whoever you were calling was coming to the wedding!

The frugality of the Morantz family eventually paid off. One day, Fannie and I got on a streetcar and went downtown. "I have to go to the bank, Gloria. You come with me." I didn't want to stay alone because I already knew I would be leaving Montreal in the not-too-distant future and I dreaded that day. At the bank, Fannie made a cash withdrawal. They had been saving money to buy their own house! The teller handed her money and I remember her stuffing some of the bills into her bra! This was the deposit for their house in NDG (Notre Dame de Grace, a more upscale neighborhood), on 4960 Montclair. This was the house I would not ever live in but would visit many times.

I was generally healthy but could not avoid childhood illnesses. I must have had my first such illness, whooping cough, as a five- or six-year-old in Poland. In Europe, if you had measles or chicken pox, you were quarantined. Was I running away from someone or something, being chased, perhaps to be isolated from others because of my cough? It was frightening! My second childhood illness, the measles, was upsetting for an entirely other reason. I was full of itchy rashes and had to stay home from school. No school? I started to get dressed as usual and began to scream. "I'm going! I have to go to school! I have to go! I'm fine! I feel okay!" I lost that fight. Fannie stayed up all night with me so I wouldn't scratch my face and get scars.

Despite her taking-care-of-business attitude, Aunt Fannie was caring. I still refer to her as Aunt Fannie and always have. Actually, it would be more accurate to call her Mother Number Three.

She was also astute in helping me become more self-confident and secure. She found ways to guarantee that this would, indeed, happen. One of these instances was really a very ordinary event for someone else, but for me it was uncomfortable. Shirley and Jack lived a streetcar ride away. The streetcar stopped near their apartment building. They had new twins, Arlene and Leslie, and I wanted to visit those adorable babies. Fannie was not always available to go with me, so she taught me how to go there on the streetcar by myself. She walked me to the streetcar, made me board the correct one, and sit in the front. She boarded and sat in the back, pretending she didn't know me. We rode the whole route separately until it was time to get off. I got off first, and then she followed. I got to the right building! From then on, I could go by myself! An accomplishment!

Around the same time period, about a year and a half after I arrived in Montreal, there was another accomplishment. It wasn't mine but had worldwide lasting significance. On Friday, May 14, 1948, David-Ben-Gurion announced the creation of the State of Israel. This four o'clock news on the radio filled Uncle Abie with unbridled joy. I was outside on this sunny day, not comprehending the actual significance of this but participating in his joyfulness. Thinking back about this today, I wish I could tell my grandfather, Zaide Pinchus. He would be so happy to know we now have our own land, Eretz Yisrael! I wish he and Uncle Abie could have celebrated together.

Once again, music was evocative. The most meaningful tune at the time, in 1948, was a tune by Leo Fuld, a Yiddish version of

Tell Me Where Can I Go. A beautifully rendered English version by Steve Lawrence also exists. I'm not sure if it was part of Abie's vinyl record collection, but I heard it on the radio. The English words are "Tell me where I can go? There's no place I can see, where to go, where to go, every door is closed for me." The Yiddish words were written by a poet who died in the Warsaw ghetto in 1942. They are "*Vu aheen zol ich gein, ver ken entfern meer, vee tsu gein, vie tsu gein, siz farshlosen yeder teer.*" Yes, every door was closed for us. Thinking about our homeland now, how differently things might have turned out if we had somewhere to go from 1938 to 1945. No nation at the Evian Conference in 1938 was willing to take in Jews except for the Dominican Republic. How many lives could have been saved? How many scientists, statesmen, artists, and musicians could have enriched humanity?

CHAPTER 2

ADJUSTING, DEVELOPING

I don't remember how it happened or how long it took, but eventually I had friends; they were Rita, Anita, Bernard, Pemeline, and Irving—the only one who lived further away from the school in a very posh neighborhood. We had a club on Friday nights and met at the school to hang out, dance, buy *karnatzels,* and enjoy them together. (If you've ever tasted Montreal's smoked meat, a cross between corned beef and pastrami to me, this deli experience is represented in a long cigar-shaped, garlic and salt-seasoned sausage-like delicacy called a *karnatzel*).

I became the president of the club. Some of my friends called me Gorgl because I supposedly had a long neck. (A *gorgl* is a chicken neck traditionally cooked in fricassee). Or it could have been a play on my names, Gloria and Gitl. I didn't mind. Once, we had a dance contest. I won the Jitterbug contest with Bernard! I loved getting dressed up and wearing my brown suede ankle strap shoes, so I looked forward to clubbing every week.

So the time with the Morantz's kept increasing, from three and a half weeks to three and a half months and eventually to three and a half years. (I was recently told that bureaucratic issues sometimes lengthened the stays of the orphans.) They only expected me to be there for about three weeks. How did they feel having this traumatized, peculiar, and brooding little immigrant girl living with them for such a long time? Did they feel put upon? Did they wish she would leave already?

Once again, I was blessed with caring, supportive strangers, who became close family. They worked on my traumas and peculiarities, loved me, and helped me to grow. I did not need the most recent phone conversation with Shirley and Rita to confirm that they considered me part of their family. I felt it during my entire stay in Montreal.

My first Purim at home costume *was* a Queen Esther costume made for me by Jack Ginsberg, Fannie's son-in-law. Jack was important not only for costume making. He was my mentor and helped to shape me as an adult. Many years later, on June 16, 2003, I was with him as he took his last breath. I recall that moment, and my thoughts about him.

I once called him my brother-in-law. Years later, I called him my cousin Jack from Canada. In truth, he was not related to me, but he became much more than a family member. He was the husband of my new sister, Shirley.

Standing near the hospital bed, I recalled him as he used to be, the handsomest man I had ever seen. A Canadian Clark Gable, he had jet-black wavy hair, a straight nose, a seemingly perpetual bright smile unaffected by the obvious gold filling on the bottom left side of his mouth, and a neatly trimmed black mustache. He was an elegant gentleman. He walked into a room, and everyone stared—a presence.

He loved music. When he came back from New York one summer, he brought with him two records of popular musicals, *Kiss Me Kate* and *South Pacific*, not yet available in Montreal. Then he would hum *Some Enchanted Evening* as he sat sketching the dress styles he had seen in New York on his business trip.

Now in the Montreal Jewish General Hospital, this was the same man, yet very different. His pale, aged face, still quite handsome, was visible above the blanket. At age eighty-four, his once jet-black hair was now white, wiry, and very short. His gnarled hands were crossed on top of the cover just below his abdomen and occasionally twitched. The oxygen tube in his nose barely missed touching the visible bone, broken during childhood, in his right nostril. His labored breathing included a detectable gurgling sound coming from his throat. I count my riches by the people in my life. I knew I was just about to get poorer.

It was a gray, sunless late afternoon. The room still had an antiseptic smell from an earlier cleaning. His wife, Shirley, and his daughter Arlene were in the room. His son, Leslie, was pacing the hall.

"Rewind the tape, Arlene," I said to Arlene after a nurse brought some tapes we had requested. "Your father loved this song. Let's give him his beloved melodies in his last moments." I stood there holding his cool, pale hand. And I began singing *Sunrise, Sunset* to him.

As Arlene rewound the tape to its beginning, I rewound the tape of my memories early in our relationship, some fifty-six years before.

I had arrived in Montreal a war-scarred and frightened eight-year-old child who was never allowed to be a child. I didn't know how to play pretend games or make believe. I had never dressed up in a costume, and the only pretend thing I could do was not to be who I was—Jewish—for that would kill me. I had to keep deep secrets. Since I had learned to be seen but not heard, I never started conversations. I never looked at people directly in the eye, probably fearing they might ridicule me for my crossed eyes. I hid behind an adult's coat or apron.

As I held Jack's hand and was catapulted back into the present, his legacy became so clear. A snowy day in February of 1948 was my first foray into pretending. Jack came over after a long workday, with rolls of blue and white crepe paper and a box of silver stars. After loosening his tie and rolling up his shirt sleeves, he skillfully cut out a long blouse by folding a long piece of crepe paper in half and cutting out a neck piece. The front and back were tied with a sash. Then he made a long skirt of the same color. He used pinking shears on the hem and around the sleeve opening. We both glued the stars randomly all over the outfit. He used the white paper attached onto a cardboard for the crown. We added stars to that too and pasted large rhinestone buttons onto each point. He had his mother-in-law sew the elastic on the crown and sew the seams on the skirt. Thus was fashioned my first costume. I put it on, smiled shyly, and walked proudly around the room. I was now the beautiful Queen Esther for the Jewish holiday of Purim!

The family spent the summer in Val Morin in the Laurentian Mountains. I loved the relief of the water from the boiling sun but was afraid to go into the lake past the level of my knees. Jack encouraged this water-phobic child to kick, put her head under the water, breathe, and eventually become a swimmer. "Take a deep breath, and then make bubbles as you exhale! See, you can do it. The water is your friend! It will hold you up." Once when I got out of the water and felt chilly, he gave me his brown stretched-out t-shirt to put on, and then took out his movie camera yelling, "Come on, champ! Smile!" I now swim at least twice a week all year, sometimes seventy-two laps (a mile) at a time!

In his prime, he could transform a plate of *hors d'oeuvres* into a work of art; he could design a beautiful dress; he used pastels and oil points to draw gorgeous flowers for tranquil water scenes. I remember being awed by the oil that hung above his living room couch. I had never known anyone who actually painted something worthy of a space on a wall! In fact, except for the picture of the Holy Mother Mary above my bed in Poland, I had never even seen a painting! He encouraged me to draw. I collected cardboard rectangles inserted into men's shirts at the cleaners and used them to draw my pictures. Once, when I was frustrated trying to copy black and white ballet slippers, he suggested, "If you draw lines lightly and separate the picture into sections, it might be easier." Then he handed me some of his drawing pencils. These veined, idle, hands once could entrap beauty in a slab of marble producing sculptures worthy of exhibition space at the

MOMA. Thus "he ignited my love of art. The three paintings signed "Ginsberg" adorning my walls" continue to enrich me even today.

His throat, now gurgling with the final death rattle, once produced a rich tenor voice singing opera. A taste of refinement so painlessly bestowed upon a nine-year old, as his own toddler twins crawled all over him while he lay on the nursery-rhymed linoleum in their room and listened to Rigoletto or Carmen. My innate love of music notwithstanding, with no musical family around me and no formal musical training, how fortunate I am to have been introduced at such a young age to the beautiful music I love today.

After my leaving Montreal in 1951, we saw each other sporadically many times at family life cycle events—weddings, births, funerals, and visits through the years. We always had an immediate bonding. When I took an art course, he wanted to see my pictures on his visits; when I told him about our upcoming trip to Italy, he happily offered some sightseeing advice. "Make sure you get to the Church *San Pietro di Vincoli*. You have to see the sculpture of Moses." Our get-togethers were always comfortable with discussions about music, plays, museums, exhibits, or about his work, or my projects.

I remember the last time he visited New York with his wife Shirley to attend a bar mitzvah. They stayed at our house after their arrival and we were going to drive them to their destination the next day. That evening we sat in the living roam around a huge aromatic bowl of fruit, listening to classical music.

"That's quite a collection of CD's you have," he remarked.

"Any requests?" I asked him. He scanned the pile of CDs on the Lucite shelf.

"Oh, here's Beethoven's and Mendelssohn's Violin Concerto. Let's listen to this one."

"We just heard Yitzchak Perlman play Bruch's at Lincoln Center a few weeks ago. These are the big three. I love the sound of the violin. I always try to get at least one concert with a violinist in our subscription," I added.

"Have I ever told you about my interest in violin as a kid? I got a small violin as a gift when I was about ten or eleven. I loved plucking it and the sound intrigued me. One day I asked my father if I could get violin lessons. 'Violin lessons?' He looked at me in disbelief. 'I have no money for that, son. You'd better get yourself a paper route instead. 'So today I'm happy if I can just listen to violin concertos," he concluded wistfully.

"Really? Imagine, I might have been going to hear you at Lincoln Center!" He laughed heartily. But I didn't think that so far-fetched.

Later, he spotted a CD cover with a group dressed in blue robes. "That's you there, isn't it?" He had picked up the CD created by my synagogue choir. "You are recorded!!" he exclaimed. "Would you have an extra copy for me?"

Though Shirley, his wife, sometimes remarked, "These two have a special relationship," I had never verbally impressed upon him how important he was in transforming this scared, traumatized child to a functioning, life-loving adult.

Now as I stood in this sterile, bare hospital room singing to him, he suddenly gasped, rolled his eyes backward, relaxed, and was gone.

"Gloria, you helped him to let go. Your singing and the music did it," declared his daughter Arlene.

Through my tears, I managed a smile. Perhaps I had finally done something for him. I had helped him take his final leave- with a song from my heart.

His legacy to me: Be a child, grow, experience, appreciate beauty, develop taste, express what's in your own soul.

I let him go. Yet he is with me still.

What else do I remember about Jack and my three and a half years in Montreal? I look at a framed pastel picture of a pink rose. It has a prominent space on the wall of one of the small bedrooms in our house. It is a piece of Jack's art he gave me after I left Montreal but returned for a visit. I was catapulted back to the kitchen table at 22 Fairmount West. Fannie sent Abie's and Stanley's shirts to the cleaners. When shirts came back from the cleaners, there were cardboard rectangles placed in the middle so the shirts would be folded properly. I was excited to get those. They were my canvases. I loved to draw. This is how I was introduced to art which delights me to this day.

In the summer, the women spent the weeks in Val Morin. The men worked all week and came up on weekends. The bungalow colony belonged to the Miller family. They had two sons, Alan and Uffy. Alan was handsome, and I had a crush on him. Uffy was homely, and he had a crush on me. We played croquet, jumped rope, and swam in the lake. Those were the summers polio appeared and families were worried about their children's health. Sometimes any ache or pain caused panic. Swimming on cooler days, we were told, was dangerous.

Rita and Buzzy had many friends who also visited on the weekends. Some of their families lived in a neighboring town like Val David. One of their friend's families, the Bindners, had a store where I got my first two-piece bathing suit. Some other friends were Beadie and Teddy, Jack and Phyllis, and Dorothy and Seymour. They always included me in their rope jumping contest. When Shirley was pregnant with her twins, she also dared to jump! Fannie would admonish her: "Shirley, don't!"

I had a few playmates my age there. We had fun playing croquet, flirting with the boys, and going to the lake. I would walk into its muddy bottom, get wet and cool off, and sit on a blanket. I was afraid to put my head under the water. Jack came to the rescue. "Turn your head to the side, then into the water and make bubbles. He put his arm under my waist and patiently walked with me as I followed his instructions. "See! That's it!" Then I would run out of the water and I'd warm up. Jack's mini lessons in swimming have given me this healthy exercise habit right up to this day.

Everyone awaited the weekend, waiting for trains or buses to come. People always brought treats or news from the city. Phone calls were made in the village where there were public phones. We collected coins to be prepared.

One weekend, Jack drove up with a new black Dodge, a fluid drive. That was an event! The first car in the family! It was as though the family sprouted wings! That car was very useful when those twins arrived.

I visited in the summer (1971 or 1972) and stayed with Shirley and Jack. Shirley was very busy and excited. Leslie had a blind date with a girl named Cheryl, who his Aunt Rita knew and recommended he take her out. He had a brand-new pair of pants that needed shortening. I had nothing to do, so I shortened his trousers.

There must have been some magic to my sewing, because they subsequently got engaged, and have been married since October 22, 1972!

Back in Montreal, the Morantzs went out to play poker at a different home each week. One of the couples, the Chodeshes, had a piano. Initially, I was always hiding behind Fanny or Abie when addressed. But I was allowed to sit at the piano and pick out tunes with one finger. I remember playing the *Anniversary Waltz*, *Five Minutes More*, and a Hebrew song called *Yussa sa Yulla la*. It was my secret wish to have a piano. That wish was fulfilled when I was about forty-five, in my own home.

Abie had a collection of (vinyl) records, including some Yiddish tunes by Menashe Skulnik such as *I'm Sam the Man Who Made the Pants Too Long*. He also had a record of Aaron Lebedeff songs, which included *Rumania, Rumania*, a song I was to hear many years later in New York after I joined the Community Synagogue in Port Washington. The Cantor, Jacob Yaron, who was born in Bucharest, sang it in his golden voice better than any recording I had heard. Whenever I hear that song, or even the word Rumania in a historical context, I can't help missing the uplifting gorgeous voice of our friend, Cantor Jacob Yaron.

When Rita and Buzzy decided to marry, the wedding, February 27, 1949, was an exciting family affair. I relished even the wedding preparations. Family came in from Chicago, including cousin Miriam. For sleeping, we doubled up. I slept on two comfortable chairs adjacent to and facing each other in the living room. I was so happy I took Miriam's hands, held them in mine, and composed little circle dances that we danced together. Years later, when I visited Montreal where she now lived with her husband Dave, we both remembered that tune and sang it again!

I was thrilled to be a junior bridesmaid. It was the first time I had an opportunity to wear a gown. My Aunt Esther brought a lime green long dress with a ruffle on the bottom. It travelled all the way from New York to Montreal! I walked down the aisle with Rita's cousin Rechia who was around my age. I loved to dance and at that wedding I had my fill, dancing with adults who would humor me, dancing the jitterbug, the *kozatzki*, the *hora*, the waltz, and the polka. While I knew no specific steps, I felt the beat, loved the music, and loved moving my body to the rhythm. I still love to dance.

That wedding made Buzzy my brother-in law. Only his title had changed. He was still the same funny, accommodating, and kind person I treasured before and after his death. The last time I saw Buzzy, many years later, was at his granddaughter Michelle's weddings. We had our last dance.

Buzzy died November 28, 2000. It was a busy Thanksgiving time and I was unable to attend his funeral. I went to Montreal to be with Rita after the *shiva* (mourning period). But I wrote her this note about what Buzzy had meant to me.

My Reflections about Buzzy Shapiro

How do I remember Buzzy? He was one of the few people who knew me as a child, a tormented and traumatized one. He is such a part of me. I remember him courting you, Rita, or when you just became engaged. You spent the weekends in Val Morin. All your friends came and you would jump rope. He and all of your friends called me Gucia. (Some still do.) In the evening, you all went out. Buzzy loved going out!

I remember Buzzy's family and your wedding, your first apartment on Van Horne and the birth of your children. Buzzy was a consummate worker, someone who stayed at one job for over sixty years. But he always found time for playing, going out, and for having fun. He loved sports and dancing, and I had a last dance with him at Michelle's wedding. He already was exhausted and without energy but didn't allow his own discomfort to ruin the *simcha* (happy occasion) for anyone.

From his good-natured teasing to his pride in me as an adult, he made me feel tall in his presence. As recently as Michelle's wedding, I noticed him speaking to another guest at the table about me. The man was also a survivor, and Buzzy was telling him my story. Near the end of that conversation, I just caught a few of his words. "And look at that *punim* (face), she now has two kids and three grandchildren."

Buzzy exuded love. Speaking of love, is there anyone who did not love Buzzy? How could you not? When I told Craig that Buzzy was very sick and in the hospital, he said, "Oh no! I love Buzzy!" When I told Jordana that Buzzy died, she gasped "Oh no!" And I could detect the tears, even in her voice. They had met him perhaps twice, but his inner warmth and his golden heart seeped through. Miles said, "Buzzy was sunshine. We lost a special person."

I remember Buzzy coming to New York on business so many years ago before I was married. We would meet at a restaurant where he always treated me to a lovely dinner, and we'd just talk about anything at all, but mostly about his family and my activities.

To say he loved his family is a gross understatement. His life was dedicated to providing for all of you, and to seeing that the life you lived was the life you loved to live. He had such pride in your accomplishments.

Was there anything any of his children, or you, Rita, wanted that he would not gladly give? Rita, you were his queen, in beauty unsurpassed, always on a pedestal. You were the jewel on his arm, and no jewel was too expensive or impossible for you to receive. Generosity was his middle name. We all felt it just being around him.

To me it seemed as though Buzzy was incapable of speaking loudly or angrily. He always peppered his remarks with a bit of pig Latin, which he actually taught me when I still lived in Montreal. He had a sense of humor that was delicious. Always looked at the bright side, and when you were with him, he gave you his undivided attention. You knew he was listening.

The beautiful combination of a strong soul with a soft heart drew so many to him. In his work and in his recreation, he was a magnet that attracted a myriad of people. It will be hard to measure the throngs of friends and acquaintances who will flock to say their last goodbyes and the numbers that will visit you during this difficult week. But if he could see it all, he would probably be surprised and amazed that this is actually a tribute to him. His humility could not fathom it.

Yet when I think of Buzzy, I think of celebration. He would want us to celebrate all that he had accomplished, all the people he has touched and all the good works he has done. He would want us to eat out, spend money, have a good time, dance, and joke. He would want life to go on—the way he always loved to live it.

Buzzy, you have left a legacy of love and vibrant life. You have provided well for your family, for your beloved Rita, for your children and grandchildren. You have left all of us whose paths have crossed with yours richer and better people. You have left us with special, unique memories that will never fade, and you have demonstrated goodness that can never be erased. You have left us all too soon, and we are bereft. But the world is a better place because you were in it. May you rest in peace, dear Buzzy. We will miss you deeply and eternally.

Buzzy Shapiro, April 2004

Esther and Max visited frequently during my three and a half years in Montreal. They developed a nice friendship with Fannie and Abie Morantz. Both couples were from Eastern Europe, were in the same line of work—the meat business—and easily communicated in Yiddish and English. But I really never warmed to my Aunt Esther and Uncle Max Bernstein as I had to the Morantzs. It's possible that distance played a part in that coolness. After all, Abie was physically present to go over my Hebrew homework with me and helped me read from the *Tanach*. Fannie began to teach me independence and instilled confidence in me. She allowed me to be the traumatized child that I was but worked assiduously to develop strength and confidence to get me out of that trauma.

I spoke English and understood it. I had friends. I had family. I was growing, becoming who I was meant to be. I liked this nest.

Then the dreaded news arrived. The bureaucratic machine that had turned three and a half weeks into three and a half years finally began working and I could now go to the USA. I was to leave the Morantz. Another country, another family, another loss. (Show small document: came as an "alien" approved for permanent residence in USA April 5, 1951) here.

I didn't want to eat. I didn't smile. I just moped and cried. The family tried to cheer me up. Whenever possible, they treated me to the movies, to the circus, prepared the dishes I liked best, and took me for a treat at a restaurant or for ice cream. They kept telling me what a wonderful place New York was. Aunt Esther and Uncle Max are rich, they assured me. "You'll have everything you want," they asserted. I was not convinced, but I had no choice. My friends in school gave me an autograph book where they wished me good luck. Uncle Abe wrote in it in Yiddish: "Maybe one day we'll rejoice at your wedding." They kept that promise.

This family had given me back my religion, my childhood, and the freedom to grow into who I was meant to be. They gave me a sense of normalcy. The three and half years had been a time of learning, developing, and thriving. A time of attachment, security, and love. But once again, the little bird had to fly away from that cozy nest. Again it was a time of leaving and grieving.

1. Aunt Fannie and Uncle Abie in front of 22 Fairmount West, Montreal

2. Gucia and Reschia, junior bridesmaids at Rita and Buzzy's wedding
3. Arlene and Leslie, Shirley and Jack's twins
4. Jack Ginsberg
5. Miles and Gloria flanked by Shirley (left) and Rita (right) at Michelle's wedding
6. (JPS) Jewish Peoples School on Waverly Street, where I became a polyglot, learning English, French, Hebrew and Yiddish.
7. Mr. Wiseman, the principal who was kind, always smiling -- and knew every child's name and background.
8. Mr. Wilchesky,-- My tall teacher, with a beautiful voice, who sang in the Choir at the Fairmount Shul

CITATIONS PART 3—MONTREAL

1. https://www.google.com/#q=origin+of+eishet+chayil+a+wom-an+of+valor Rita concluding section of The Book of Proverbs (31:10-31)
2. Goldberg, Adara. *The Alex Dwokin Canadian Jewish Archives.* File document from the United Jewish Relief Agencies Collection

PART 4

AMERICA

IMMIGRATION LAWS AND
POLICIES AFFECT SURVIVORS

T he Displaced Persons Act of 1948 permitted Europeans displaced by the war to enter the United States outside of immigration quotas. I suppose these accounts for my Aunt Norma's ability to come to USA in 1947. Still, I wonder why this didn't apply to me. Her Certificate of Identity in Lieu of Passport (single journey only) from the American Consulate General in Munich, Germany indicates she is a Polish citizen who intends to immigrate to the United States of America. According to the document, she has never been convicted of any crime—*except for* being Jewish and therefore in a concentration camp! She sailed on the Ernie Pyle from Bremen, Germany.

Just two years later, in 1950, the Internal Security Act, passed over President Harry Truman's veto, bars admission to any foreigner who is a communist or who might engage in activities "which would be prejudicial to the public interest, or would endanger the welfare or safety of the United States." Was I, at age eight, a threat to the United States, endangering the welfare or safety of the United States?

In 1952, the McCarran Walter Immigration Act, passed over President Harry Truman's veto, affirmed the national origins quota system of 1924 and limited total annual immigration to one-sixth of one percent of the population of the continental United States in 1920. The act exempted spouses and children of U.S. citizens and people born in the western hemisphere from the quota. In all of its parts, the most basic purpose of the 1924 Immigration Act was to preserve the ideal of U.S. homogeneity. Congress revised the Act in 1952.

But I came as an alien with permission for permanent residence. I was under the Polish quota, which was very small, and even then not totally used. So it took me five years to get here. Show document of my coming as an alien.

https://history.state.gov/milestones/lBZl-1936/immigrationect #1 website

Document shows I left Sweden December 12, 1947 (arrived Canada December 20, 1947=*8 days on ship) Cited in Sweden Section

CHAPTER 1

A HEARTBREAKINGLY SAD LITTLE GIRL ARRIVES AND ADJUSTS

Grand Central Station, New York, April 5, 1951. The train from Montreal arrives in the morning. Among the passengers is a twelve-year-old girl and her "aunt", Fannie Morantz. It was an all-night trip but they had a couchette, which was a sleeping loft with a long curtain dividing the aisle from the makeshift bed. So it was only a fitful night, not a sleepless one.

From my adopted sister-in-law, Tobi, who continues, even today at age 91, to be a mentor for me, I got the description of me as I arrived: "a heartbreakingly sad little girl."

Yes, the house at 1724 Popham Avenue in the Bronx was beautiful, with a back yard that had a shuffle ball court, a garage for the Oldsmobile, three bathrooms, (even one in the attic), a basement, a sun parlor, and a bedroom just for me. It was an imposing brick house flanked by two tall apartment buildings. By any standard in 1951, and even today, it was commodious and desirable. It was very different from the walk-up apartment I had just left at 22 Fairmount West, in Montreal.

To keep the upholstery clean, Esther had plastic covers on the nice couch and chairs. Actually, it was at the far end of the living room, so we practically never used it. When it was hot and we had company and wanted to use it, our skin stuck to the plastic, so a clean white sheet was placed on top of the plastic. Therefore, one could not really tell if the couch was elegant or not, or worth pre-serving! In some parts of the house that were heavily trafficked, there were plastic runners on the carpet as well.

Once more, with no input from me, with no questioning, com-forting, or explaining, I was thrust into unfamiliar surroundings. New visitors, new friends, a new school, and most importantly, new relationships with my unknown family members. Blood relatives do not necessarily guarantee ease, comfort, and love. Aunt Fannie was with me for a few days to soften the impact of the strangeness. She seemed to be on very friendly terms with Esther and Max. They greeted each other warmly, speaking mostly in Yiddish—a language I now understood and no longer needed to hide.

Within days I met all the close relatives, basically my cousins who were eventually to become my brothers: Sam, age thirty-two, and his wife Phyllis and their chubby son, Howard, around seven years old; Phil, twenty-nine, and his wife Tobi and their adorable sons Paul and Richard, around five and three; and Erwin, twenty-two, and his wife May, and their baby daughter, Joyce. Though they were already adults with their own families when I met them, they were the product of two very indulgent parents, Max and Esther. Erwin had received a Chevy convertible for his sixteenth birthday which he wasn't supposed to drive in the city until he turned eighteen, but he did; Phil, after he had been discharged from the Marines, went to NYU downtown. He didn't want to commute on the subway from the Bronx, so his parents got him an apartment in the village; and Sam, who wanted to be a doctor, couldn't get into medical school in New York with the name Bernstein, so after his Air Force discharge, Max arranged to offer some money so he was accepted but because of his debilitating, recurring (twice weekly) migraine headaches, had to drop out and work in the family meat business. (This injury was caused by his plane being shot down, flying one of his fifty-four mis-sions). I don't think he ever got over the loss of his friend, Pudgy, whom he always mentioned when referring to that period in his Air Force career.

I don't remember any specific early conversations with them, but I do remember the many family get-togethers. One of the family favorites, besides steak dinners, was herring! Pickled herring, matches herring, bony smelly herring as I remembered it from Sweden! I usually walked out of the room when it was served!

Though I hated those meals, eventually, the understanding and caring of my new brothers and sisters-in-law made my stay with the Bernstein's bearable. I was assured of that by Tobi when I visited after school and expressed my misery about having to leave Montreal. She recalled: "We were in my living room on 180th St. You had come over after school. I think it was before the twins were born (1952 or early 1953). I said something about understanding how difficult life with Esther was after living with the Morantz family. That brought on your tears. And in comforting you, I told you that we would always be there for you if you needed us." They were true to their word.

P.S. 26 was a long walk from the house on Popham Avenue. But on my first day there, Uncle Max gave me a ride in the two-tone green Oldsmobile 88. We pulled up in front of the yard and I said good-bye to him. I had been at the school the week before when Aunt Esther brought me in to register. I had arrived in New York on April 5th, so I was actually coming to the school for the first time at the end of April, near the end of the school year. I was turning twelve in May, entered the last two months of sixth grade, the same grade I had been at JPS. When my uncle pulled away, I noticed that the yard was almost completely empty. I saw one or two students entering through the heavy brown metal doors. I thought it somewhat strange to see an empty schoolyard in the morning, but I thought I was early so I waited a while expecting to see the yard fill up as time passed. I leaned against gray metal fence holding my notebook and pencil case and the yellow registration card. It was a pleasant April day, bright sunshine on the wall of the school building, while the other side of the yard was in shade. The mild breezes were harbingers of spring.

After standing there for about fifteen minutes and with the yard still empty, I began to feel very uncomfortable. Just then I saw another student walking over to me. "Hey, kid, do you go to this school?" he asked. "Yes," I answered, raising my eyelids. "Well, you better go in. You're already late!"

Really? I didn't have a watch. But would my aunt and uncle have made such an error and taken me to school late? I walked in not knowing whether I was more embarrassed or frightened. New school, new teacher, new students, not one familiar face. And to make a grand entrance no less. I walked on the first floor looking for the room number on the yellow card. It was not anywhere I was walking. I finally found the room on the second floor. The door was open, and the teacher was explaining the work on the board. I slowly moved toward the doorway and hesitated. The teacher noticed me, stopped mid-sentence and smiled, saying: "Oh, please come in. You must be Gloria. Boys and girls, we have a new girl. She is from Canada. Let's all welcome her." A cacophony of greetings erupted. *Hi, Gloria; Hello; Hiya; Hi there.* I thought to myself, Americans are really friendly, as I had been told.

I managed to get through the morning work with a little extra explanation from the teacher. At recess, the kids, intrigued by my Canadian accent, all wanted to hear me speak. "Say p-y-j-a-m-a-s, say g-a-r-a-g-e," and so on. So now I not only had no friends, had no familiarity with the curriculum, had no clue where the rooms were, but I also spoke differently. Yet, I was going to survive this. Perhaps it was good being late. The teacher had time to prepare her students for this strange creature.

At least I didn't have to handle the lunchroom that first day. I was going to my cousin Sam and Phyllis for lunch. Fortunately, Phil and Sam lived about one block from the school, on 180th Street, across from the NYU uptown campus. That is where the Hall of Fame statues of famous people would enchant my friends and me on Rosh Hashanah and school holidays. I was going to complete the next two months of sixth grade in my new school. I had never spent an entire school year in a grade 'til seventh grade at PS. 82, Macomb's Junior High School in the Bronx. To this day, I don't really understand decimals. And now it was about to happen—my first whole year in one grade, the seventh, next year. But first a medical procedure.

On the Grand Concourse, there was a stately professional building called the Lewis Morris where Dr. Gartner, an ophthalmologist, had his office. When I had arrived in Montreal, the immigration officers threw away my glasses, claiming they were totally wrong for me and my crossed eyes. Esther insisted that Dr. Gartner was a very good doctor and would straighten my eyes as he had done for her Phil many years before. So before the school year ended, I was brought to Monteflore Hospital to have the surgical procedure. Knowing this was surgery, I assumed I was going to be put to sleep and wake up when the procedure was completed. That was not to be. I had to keep my eye open so they could move the parts (which looked like rubber bands) and straighten or stretch the eye muscles. I remember some words during the surgery like *pontocaine* (a local anesthetic). I had to wear a patch for about a week afterwards and insert some drops. Then I saw my eyes were no longer crossed. Strabismus gone! Finally, I would no longer be called Cockeyed Jennie!

While attending PS. 26 to finish sixth grade, I often went to Phyllis and Sam's for lunch. She made me cottage cheese on top of a slice or two of canned pineapple with a maraschino cherry on top. The first time I saw that, I felt so well treated! It looked special and beautiful to me! Pineapple and cottage cheese. But the cherry did not taste like the one in that distant long-ago garden.

Sam and Phyllis lived on the lower floor of the two-family house, and Tobi and Phil lived on the top floor. As I entered the main foyer, the biggest attraction here was a large, colorful fish tank with tropical fish—angel fish, guppies, and others, and unfamiliar tiny structures like coral and rock formations. I saw the bubbling water and the multicolored creatures swimming all around. Sam cleaned the fish tank, sprinkled the fish food, and the fish pounced at each sprinkle. Subsequently, at art class in JHS 82, I drew pictures of fish tanks with India ink and pens, clarifying perspective. When my granddaughter Lexi asks me to draw a picture for her, I sometimes revert to drawing a fish tank with fish.

But at 1724 Popham Avenue especially for the first two or three years after my arrival, I remember very few happy times. At first, many people came over to see the new little girl who just arrived. I was shy, but I was on show. Esther was often sick and upstairs in bed with pneumonia, or a cold, and I stood against the wall silently, sometimes forcing a smile, not knowing what to say or how to respond to their questioning. I did not know how to answer: "How does it feel to be a New Yorker now?"

Initially, I could do nothing right. Why did I put the soap there and why not here? What did you do with . . .? I ironed my own clothes and sometimes even house items like tablecloths. Why didn't you iron that? It seemed I never did enough or never did it well enough. I don't remember Esther ever hugging me or acknowledging my feelings about missing Fannie and Able or encouraging me with possibilities of going to visit them. No. She did not know how to treat a depressed child on the cusp of becoming a teenager. I took care of my room and my clothes. I was sometimes embarrassed to bring friends over because Esther wasn't very friendly, had an accent, and Max fell asleep on the oversized, velvet, maroon chair in the living room and sometimes snored. While my friend Linda was excited about me having a beautiful house, a beautiful room, and new bedroom set, I was envious that her parents were educated—her father a pharmacist and her mother a college graduate.

Much later, I realized that Max and Esther did not know how to be my parents. I was too young for them; they were too old for me. And I was not a toddler like their grandchildren, whom Esther doted on. I was twelve, and to me, it seemed I was of no interest to her.

Our flawed relationship notwithstanding, I cannot, however, discount Esther and Max's generosity in taking me out of Europe, supporting me through high school and college and beyond, and taking on the role of being my parents. She was concerned about my health and well-being. As time went on, our relationship calmed down and I felt less resentful toward her. Perhaps it was my becoming a teenager that made the first few years more difficult. We did make sure she was taken care of in her older age, securing an apartment for her opposite ours after Max died, and later having her live with us in our home in Port Washington. Though she lived in a facility in New Jersey after she fell down the stairs and injured herself in Sam's house, I hope she did feel my gratitude when she lived with us where her medical needs and general comfort were always considered and attended to. She was treated with respect by her son-in-law, my husband Miles, and had her two youngest grandchildren in the same house. Though she was not especially kind and affectionate as I expect grandmas to be, and our son told us some of his friends actually were afraid of her, it's unfortunate she could not enjoy what I, now a grandmother, know—grandchildren are the best medicine! Esther died in 1984.

Max was more affectionate, hugging me or planting a kiss on my head. He gave me an allowance of $1.00 a week. Max often asked me, "Do you need more money?" I always said no. I had learned good lessons on being frugal in Montreal. I even saved enough to sometimes buy myself a piece of clothing. (I didn't like Esther's taste in clothes for me.) I made do, even walking from Sheridan Avenue (instead of taking a bus) where Max's uncle Philip Dutkowitz, (Uncle Phil) and his red-headed wife Goldie and their daughter Cookie, who was my age, lived. I was very close with Cookie and slept over there many times. Goldie was comedy personified! She was Rumanian and even made us *mamalige* (a Rumanian type of porridge) for breakfast. Whenever there was a life cycle event such as a wedding or *bar mitzvah*, Cookie and I would dance together almost all night! Max always commented on my energy level. "She is so active! Doesn't sit still for a minute." People say that to me even today, in my late seventies!

CHAPTER 2

A New Family, Adjusting, Learning, and Teaching

Uncle Phil was Max's mother Sima Pearl's twin brother. When she died, Max's father David, called Zaide, a beloved grandpa to all, moved in with us. I remember him living in the attic for some time, and then in the back bedroom on the second floor. One evening, we were eating dinner in the lovely dinette area of the kitchen wallpapered with white and red roses. It was a traditional *Shabbat* meal—chicken fricassee, soup, roast chicken, and always tasteless vegetable from a can. But the fricassee with *feeselach* (chicken feet) was delicious. It was Esther's specialty, along with her stuffed cabbage.

I began to speak to her. "Mmm, Aunt Esther, I like the fricassee. Isn't it good, Uncle Max?" Then Zaide, speaking softly in Yiddish, corrected me. "I know they are your aunt and uncle. But now they are no longer that. They are your mother and father. So call them Mama and Papa." From that day on, they became Mom and Pop. He helped me overcome my resistance. The quiet, unobtrusive correction and wisdom of old age. Is this part of a new normal?

It was late March 1952, and I would be thirteen in two months. My Aunt Esther, whom I now called mom, was in Florida, due to return in about two weeks in time for Passover. It was up to me to do the cooking for my Uncle Max, now "Pop," and his father, my eighty-five-year-old Zaide. The usual Friday night dinner was chicken and soup with noodles, with an appetizer of chopped eggs and onions. Pop wasn't home from work yet, and Zaide had already walked to the nearby synagogue. The meal was ready, and I was setting the table for the three of us.

The doorbell rang repeatedly.

"There's fire in your window upstairs! You better call the Fire Department!" a stranger frantically shouted as she pointed to the upstairs window.

I rushed upstairs two steps at a time, and sure enough, the gauze curtains blowing out of the window were aflame, obviously ignited by the Sabbath candles Zaide had lit on the small round table in his room. I see that so far only the curtains were aflame, so thinking I could put this out myself, I run to the kitchen and grab the biggest pots I could find, fill them with water in the bathtub upstairs, and proceed to pour it on the burning curtains. After about three or four potfuls, I succeed in quenching the fire. At least the firemen wouldn't have to ruin the whole room with their hoses, I think. But then I remembered hearing that you should have the Fire Department come just in case there are embers left that could ignite. When they arrive, I tell them what I had done, and after checking the room, and writing a short report, they leave.

Now I am seething. In my rush to put out the fire, I had put my emotions on hold as I worked speedily with nervous energy to put out the fire. But now I felt the anger rise against my serene, soft-spoken *Zaide*. I would tell him! How stupid to open a curtained window near burning candles! What was he thinking? Any ten-year-old would know that was dangerous! The minute he came home I would let him have it!

I hear the key turning in the lock. Zaide enters.

"Gut Shabbes, Gut Shabbes" (Good Sabbath) he says in his meek, innocent voice.

I stand mute. I cannot utter anything except *"Gut Shabbes."* He had completely defused my anger.

Ever since my love of music had been ignited in Montreal, I wished for a piano and piano lesson. In the context of a relaxing evening, I simply asked if we could get a piano. "No, we can't buy it now. It's too expensive," I was told. Possibly Max had had some financial reversals with the slaughterhouse which he owned on Frelinghuysen Avenue in Newark, New Jersey. Though disappointed, I didn't pursue the request any more. From an early age, I learned not to question, to do and accept what I was told. Within a few months, though, Esther got a new mink stole. I guess I was disappointed, even angry. About thirty-two years later, I got my Mason Hamlin piano, and for a short time took piano lessons at the same time as our daughter, Jordana. Age forty-four was too late for me to develop any piano skill. My fingers were short, and I was not gifted but would have loved to know how to play well. Not being musically trained on an instrument or in voice is a regret I continue to have.

I loved going to McCombs Junior HS 82. It was a departmental program, and I had a different teacher and subject every forty-five minutes. Once a week we had a library period when we could take home books and return them the following week. Somehow, I got the impression (mistakenly) that I had to read two books a week! I took this very seriously and followed the rule as I had learned in my earlier life. This error actually proved very beneficial for me. Within five months, my reading level skyrocketed from seventh grade level to ninth grade level!

Not only did my reading level get higher in ninth grade. After two years in this free country, my awareness of anti-Semitism also increased. I finished junior high and wanted to get a summer job. The best way to find one was to read the Sunday New York Times ads and appear for an interview for that particular job description as soon as possible after the ad appeared. I did exactly that, arriving before the company opened the next morning to apply for the receptionist position. I was told: "The job is already taken." I was fourteen. My last name was Bernstein. Now, sixty-four years later, I still remember that event.

I excelled in French, possibly because of my head start with it in Montreal. But I actually loved the sound and the melodious aspects of its pronunciation. I loved listening to Edith Piaf singing *Je ne regrette rien* or *Padam Padam Padam*. My teacher, Mr. Middleton, not only taught French but loved opera and would discuss the talents of Robert Merrill and Roberta Peters. Of course, my favorite opera is also French: *Carmen*. Merrill and Peters were a pair not only professionally but were husband and wife. I remember going to hear them at Lewisohn Stadium on the City College campus with my new sister-in-law, Phyllis. Again, my introduction to opera ignited by Jack in Montreal now blossomed. Eventually, my ability in French merited the French Medal at junior high school graduation.

My arithmetic problems from Montreal seemed to vanish as I took more advanced math. I was amazed with my love of and proficiency in algebra. I had an excellent algebra teacher, Miss Sheridan. I still use some of her suggestions for estimation that she introduced us to. My science teacher, Mrs. Grey, made experiments and results clear and understandable. She related it to our everyday lives, so that I could understand why a metal spoon in soup conducts the heat and heats the soup longer, why wearing white in summer keeps us cooler because the rays of the sun are not absorbed as quickly as by dark colors! Mrs. Hannon, the art teacher, taught us various procedures with pen and India ink such as crosshatching and perspective. According to my report cards, I did fairly well in school. My grades were in the 90s and high 80s. I credit my fine teachers for some of my academic success.

CHAPTER 3

FINALLY, FRIENDS

M y friendship with Linda Dorn deepened as we travelled as a class to each subject, saw each other all day, and shared many interests. We visited each other's houses often and both had an interest in writing for the junior high school magazine, *The Scholarship*. We became associate editors of the magazine the year we graduated. I remember sitting in Linda's apartment with a sign "inspiration please" overlooking our efforts. I remember writing a short poem "Ups and Downs." This was my first "published" poem. Both of us wrote a "Last Will and Testament of the Graduating Class of June '54." In my older age, I have also written lyrics about people using tunes of familiar songs, such as "Those Were the Days." Sometimes I rib people, "You better be nice to me, or I'll write a song about you!"

At Linda's house, writing for *The Scholarship*

When it was time for high school, I had no idea about special schools, New York City schools like Stuyvesant or Hunter that required written entrance exams. But my brothers had other ideas. My fragmented schooling resulted in mixed intelligence test results. It's possible that at the time some tests were culturally biased. Coming from Canada, I knew about Champlain, the Canadian provinces, and other bits of Canadian history. But I don't remember even knowing that George Washington was the first president of the United States! Or perhaps I wasn't really smart enough to get at least a 115 score which I think was necessary to qualify just to take the entrance exam for special schools such as Hunter College HS, or Bronx High School of Science. The guidance counselor at PS 82 would not allow me to take the test. Enter my adopted oldest brother, Sam. "What do you mean she can't? I don't care what they want! Do you know what this kid went through? Seventh grade was her first full year in one grade! In three years she went through six grades!!! You allow her to take that test!!" She did. Hunter College High School was my next school. My reaction and my brothers': Hurray! But also some angst. Now that I'm allowed to take the test, I better pass it!

I made many friends in junior high school. Three boys, Sammy, Dave, and George; and three girls, Linda, Marcy, and I would often have snowball fights in my back yard. Sometimes we had parties, including New Year's Eve parties in my basement. I had to be sure we cleaned up the basement and left it the way we found it. At other get-togethers, Max's big roll of butcher paper was convenient for us to draw on. We enjoyed doing that, especially after I got a new set of charcoals! Life was becoming more predictable. My early years were receding and receding, and must have gone deeply into my subconscious. And I don't remember ever discussing my really early life with my "parents," perhaps only my most recent life in Montreal because I did take trips to Montreal.

Linda's father, Harry Dom, had the pharmacy in the neighborhood, Dorn's Pharmacy, and was a beloved member of the community. You could ask him about certain conditions or medical issues, and he would recommend over the counter remedies. Some people even called him Doc.

Around Christmas time, Linda and her mother went to the store to decorate it for the holiday season. Linda became very skilled at using beautiful wrappings and tying special bows on the fake gifts that would be in the shop window. Linda's parents would often include me in her birthday celebrations. Her father didn't drive so they frequently used taxis. One year, we all went to Radio City Music Hall by taxi to see *Call Me Madam* starring Ethel Merman all the way downtown from the Bronx in a taxi! We would go for an ice cream treat afterwards, sometimes we would go to Rushmeyers on University Avenue and occasionally even to Krums on the Concourse and Fordham Road. I felt special.

We formed a club called the Teen-ettes and had dark green and Chartreuse sweater jackets made. I belonged. In the summer, we went to Long Beach where Uncle Max (now Pop) owned an apartment building and a two-family house. I loved the beach, rode my bike, and walked on the boardwalk in the evening with Cookie and Linda. Cookie's mother said we were going fishing (looking for boys!). That was true!

Strict observance of Judaism at the Bernstein's was something reserved for the High Holidays and Passover Seders even though Esther lit candles on Friday night and Yiddish was spoken most of the time. Esther and Max had tickets for the High Holidays at the Shield of David services nearby. I could actually have a regular seat there. But I preferred to go with Linda's family to their temple and sit on the window sill with her. They had a choir there which broke up the length of the service and added variety and pleasure for me. I felt grateful to have that choice. Linda's friendship was joyful for many reasons. I don't ever remember an angry moment with her, and also admired her parents whom I got to know and love.

One of the saddest memories of that friendship is the time I went to her house on a school day in December 1959 to get to Hunter College (now Lehman) as usual; I barely reached her building when I saw Linda and her mother, Cynthia Dorn, walking up the hill. *Something was terribly wrong,* I thought. As they approached, I saw the tear-stained eyes. I was familiar with loss. My fears were confirmed. They were returning from the hospital where Harry Dorn had died during the night. Too young. I carried this sorrow with me to school that day and afterwards. It seemed the whole neighborhood was in mourning. Everyone missed Doc Harry Dorn.

My high school years were filled with study, looking for dates, dating, and activities with friends. Hunter was an all-girls school so to augment our social life, we had dances with all-boys schools such as Stuyvesant and Brooklyn Tech. I remember those dances as being a bit uncomfortable with boys on one side of the room and girls on the other. Girls waited to be asked to dance. There was also cutting in, where you were already dancing with someone and another boy came and asked you if you would dance with him so your partner had to find another if you agreed!

Linda and I had a long walk to the subway. We would frequently meet our Latin teacher, Dr. Corrigan. She seemed so old to us then, (probably below sixty), and we felt uncomfortable conversing with her. Sometimes people offered her a seat, but she usually refused. In the classroom, I was petrified of her. She called each of us by our second name, so I was Miss Beuhnstein. (She pronounced it that way). She would hand out board slips which required the recipients to go to the blackboard and write the translation or conjugation recorded on the slip. Everyone would be able to see how ill-prepared or stupid we were! Still, she was an amazingly thorough teacher, bringing in examples of words from newspapers or magazines to show how Latin has influenced English. My grades in Latin were mostly 95–98!

I became a big sister to younger Hunterites, was on the "Knocks and Boosts" (short phrases about each graduate) committee and tried to stay fit doing the Royal Canadian Air Force Exercises. But at no time in high school did I speak to anyone about my earlier life. Recently, June 4, 2017, I went to my sixtieth Hunter High School reunion. It was a wonderful event with conversations about my early European experiences with several long-ago friends. They were shocked at how well-hidden those were during high school. My grades and academic performance were not stellar, but acceptable, with marks in the 80s and 90s in a college preparatory school with many brilliant achievers.

Back during the Hunter High years, my friends were amazed I could stand on my head! Today I would be amazed if I could do that! I also loved folk dancing, and my good friend Sunny Lippman, (now

Sunny Hudes) and I went to the Ninety-Second Street once a week to do Israeli folk dancing, taught by Fred Berk who had a club foot and could only describe the steps. He had a demonstrator assistant to show us how to dance those steps. I always looked forward to those nights of Israeli music, which was the impetus for my collecting records of Israeli music that I still cherish.

CHAPTER 4

EDUCATION

By junior year, conversations began to center around college choices. Coming from the type of old-fashioned home I was from, I knew I wasn't going out of town and would even have to fight to go to college at all. Enter my strong-willed, dogmatic brother Phil. "Of course, she's going to college. And I think she should apply to Brandeis!" Max's eyes nearly crossed. "Why does she need college? She can be a secretary; she'll get married and have children. She doesn't need college." Phil gave up on Brandeis. The compromise: I would go to Hunter College (for which you needed to have a high enough average in high school), free of board and tuition, and close to home in the Bronx.

I did not really understand at that time what a gift Hunter College was. I got an excellent liberal arts education for a $24 bursar's fee, and my books were free! After we registered for our courses, we went to the college basement and picked out the books on the shelves listed with our course number. There was a fairly daunting requirement of courses we had to take, pick a group you were in, i.e. science group, social science, arts and so forth. This had nothing to do with one's major. Every student could pick a major in any group, and then had to fulfill the major requirements. I picked the science group which required me to take four science courses. I loved science except for chemistry. I think one of the lowest grades I ever got in college was a C in chemistry. I couldn't understand the formulas or the concepts. I just struggled. My brother Sam rescued me again. Even though he was twenty years older than I, he still knew his chemistry, and helped me pass this confounding subject.

Even though by then I knew I was going to be a teacher, (since childhood I always wanted to be one) education could not be my major. I majored in English. The English major forced me to spend my holidays and weekends in the reading room of the Forty-Second Street library writing research and term papers. So today, as a member of a book club with very intelligent, well-prepared readers, I refuse to take notes on the books I read, and do not mark or require myself to analyze the writing style of authors or find examples of exemplary writing. I did enough of that. Now I can just read for pleasure, and what I remember, I remember; though I actually forget much more.

In college, I joined the service sorority Gamma Sigma Sigma. One of the requirements was that we had to perform some type of service in the community or the college, *gratis*. I remember working at Lebanon Hospital on Mt. Eden Avenue in the Bronx in the clinic that handled emotional and psychological issues. My job was to record the appointments of the patients as they left and greet them warmly when they arrived. It was an easy job and I inherited the name Gigi from one of the patients! I think the movie with Leslie Caron was out at that time, hence the reference.

But the real perk of belonging to Gamma Sigma Sigma was *APO, Alpha Phi Omega*, the service fraternity. I had at least two boyfriends I met there. We had ski trips and parties, and we had fun. I felt accepted. I could be myself. But still no one knew about my early years. I fit in, didn't want to be different, and wanted to be normal like everyone else.

My sorority sister, Brenda, and I became good friends (to this day) and she was very proactive about having a social life and meeting Mr. Right. She planned trips to various singles gathering places such as Tamiment, Green Mansions, The Tarleton, and Nantucket after college. Though I had many dates from those trips, I did not meet my husband in any of those resorts.

Even through all those times together, I never revealed my background to her. It wasn't 'til my father Max died in 1969, she said, that she actually got to know. My friend Linda who had transferred to Hunter from Buffalo never suspected the Bernstein's were not my parents, and neither did Sunny, who learned about my early life in college.

CHAPTER 5

Looking Back "The Lies I told"

People who know me would never accuse me of being dishonest, but for much of my life I was an expert and skillful liar. Breaking open the secure protective shelter of silence, happened so gradually and so naturally that I didn't even feel it to be a conscious act on my part.

It was so natural to call a stranger *Matka*, mother, for three years. It was equally easy, five years later, to refer to another unrelated woman as my mother for three and a half years. By extension, I had to perpetuate the lie and refer to her children as my sisters and brother. And when the oldest of them had her twins, it was only logical for me to call them niece and nephew, even though it meant I was a nine-year-old auntie.

But three-year-olds, five-year-olds, and even nine-year-olds can hold inner truths. Who is a mother? The one who cares for you, nurtures you, feeds you, and loves you. To me that was the truth. My *Matka* was my mother, Fannie Morantz was my mother, and Esther Bernstein was also my mother by the above definition. So there was truth in the lie I told. All the other aspects of my life with them thus became my truths.

Omission is also untruthful and is equal to lying. I would tell people I lived in Canada; I came from Montreal, and made it sound as though I had been born there. Purportedly, my father's business led me to New York.

When I look at my life through this perspective, I wonder why it came so naturally to me. No one actually told me to lie, though my *Matka* told me never to tell anyone I was Jewish. But even at a very young age, I must have evoked the strong drive of self-preservation. Somehow, I knew that if I wanted to live, I had better lie. So I did.

The lies continued even when I was in a safer time and neighborhood. Perhaps now it was another drive at work. Now I could fit in. I could have a "Dick and Jane" family, a mother, father, siblings, and an address. I could be normal, whatever that meant.

Then my parents were really too old to be my parents and my brothers were quite old to be my siblings. But something about my resolute descriptions of my family kept people from probing more deeply. Somehow, I avoided the questions that I didn't want to answer. And here again, I conjecture that I didn't want to evoke the pain associated with those answers, so I was happy not to have questions asked. In truth, it's possible I wanted to forget that painful past.

Truth, the Talmud says, is one of the three pillars upon which the world rests. But it also states that "he who saves a life, it is as though they have saved the world." So my *Matka*, Maria Kowalczyk, saved a life. So she saved the world. Could she have done so without lying that I was her daughter, her widowed cousin's child, or her illegitimate granddaughter?

Now I speak and write and seek facts about my past. I am keenly aware that even my biblical ancestors also lied. But I possess a deep sense of ethics, and no one would call me a liar. I have passed my value system on to my students and my own children.

For much of my life, I realize, I was wearing a harlequin costume of many colors and an intertwining design of many colors. Also a mask. One side was about lying and forgetting, and the other was about remembering and seeking truths. I am, at my roots, a Jewish child of many mothers, many families, residences, and many lives. These lies became truths for me. I'm not clownish or comedic, but perhaps because my lies hurt no one, and actually were intrinsically connected to saving a life, I have been strangely comfortable in this costume.

Lying: At first it saved my life, then it permitted me to be accepted.

It allowed me to be like everyone else, with the mother, father, and siblings.

It kept people from asking questions and from the pain of answering the questions.

I had the veneer of being normal.

How did I get my sense of ethics?

How did I pass and infuse my kids with a sense of values?

How did I pick an ethical partner in my life? Questions still to ponder.

CHAPTER 6

EXPANDING MY WORLD

Those were good years. I did not have any distinction like Phi Beta Kappa, or cum laude after my name when I finished my college courses. But I graduated college! I did not regard it as a big achievement at the time. When I saw the Friedmans in 2011, Arnold and Marilyn mentioned that they had told Maria when they visited her in 1978 that I had gone to college. Though she probably did not know the significance of that as she probably left school by third grade, I can imagine her pride and wistful regret that she hadn't heard from me all those years, and the little girl she rescued was not only musical and cute, but also educated. It wasn't until much later that I found out how proud Phil and Tobi were when they attended my college graduation. They felt it was a great achievement for me to have made it through such an excellent college. Their daughter Barbara, who was about eight years old then, confirmed her mother's joy: "I remember when you graduated college, but at that time, I wasn't sure I knew what that meant. I figured it must be something really special because mom was so happy and proud of you. I could hear it in her voice when she told us the news."

I don't know how Max and Esther felt about it, but we went out for a celebratory dinner. They did attend the graduation outside, and it was a beastly hot day. I think they did mention it later, to people they knew; I think they actually were proud.

I took the three-part test to become a teacher in New York City. Since I wanted to teach the elementary grades, Common Branches, I had to pass three separate sections on three different dates: a written one, an oral one, and a practical one. There were previous test examples I could study, and Linda and I spent many hours going over those questions.

The last one scared me the most. We were in front of a panel of judges as we taught a lesson to a group of students we were seeing for the first time, with scant materials we were given after describing the topic briefly. After I passed the test, I was placed by the Board of Education in a school that needed teachers. I was placed in a very challenging neighborhood in the East Bronx, into a special service school, synonymous with difficult kids.

While I had always wanted to be a teacher, I was not even remotely prepared for the demands of teaching first graders who came from very difficult home situations, sometimes taking turns wearing a pair of shoes and not having had a bed to sleep on by themselves, who had never seen a book or had one read to them. I had to calm their emotions, develop a sense of discipline in the classroom, relate to irate parents, and actually teach them basic alphabet skills that would eventually allow them to become readers. I remember the fatigue at the end of the school day. I needed to take a nap almost every day after I got home.

Those were not the only problems. While I was able to park my car very close to the school, I left school one day and found I could not start my car. I returned into the building and asked the helpful school custodian to check under the hood. He did. "You have no battery," he concluded. Someone had stolen my car battery!

A very frightening incident occurred one early morning before the children arrived at school. I was alone in the classroom writing something on the blackboard when a woman reeking of alcohol entered. She was the mother of one of my very sweet, well-behaved little girls who had been diagnosed with epileptic seizures. She had, up to that point, never had one in my room. The woman walked into my room uninvited, picked up the yard stick on the ledge of the blackboard, and announced to me firmly: "If Susan doesn't behave properly, I want you to use this on her, you hear!"

I lasted the year, became more skilled at controlling student behavior and at doing my job. I know there were many times I felt I couldn't last to the next weekend or day off. While some students were difficult to teach, I had a few who made it worth my while.

I recently found a picture of a second grader who wrote on the back of his class picture which he gave to me: "Dear Miss Bernstein, I will always do my work an (sic) behave. Love Richard." I have held on to this picture since 1961–1962.

But this is where I had to be. There were no other options, and I would not quit. My friend Judy actually developed a nervous tick and through the auspices of our understanding principal, was able to be transferred to a school in a more stable environment.

My resolve rewarded me. After about three years, a new position opened up which was much less stressful for me and more interesting for the children. Teachers had to get a prep period twice a week. That meant they had to get time off to do planning (Plan books were collected by the assistant principal) each week. So a teacher was relieved by another teacher who would teach her class. I volunteered to teach science to the students while teachers had their prep periods. I actually did not have a classroom but had a spacious closet where I kept some science materials on a wheeled cart. There was a metal door without a window. This enabled me to have some privacy. I could take my shoes off and put my head on the desk for five-minute break. The science lessons became portable. I had a chair in this closet so I could sit and plan the lessons. I tried to do hands-on experiments with air, water, seeds, and so on. I didn't have to do report cards or deal with irate parents, and the kids were more interested. We would write an experience chart about what we did and even developed some reading skills through science. This position was a relief because I didn't have to discipline unruly children. The kids enjoyed hands-on science experiments and even looked forward to this science period.

After about two years in this position, another interesting opportunity presented itself. A communiqué was circulated announcing the availability of an "Experienced Teacher Fellowship Program" sponsored by Columbia University Teachers College. It was a one-year master's degree in Supervision in Early Childhood Education which included thirty credits free, plus a one-year stipend of $4000 to make up for the salary a teacher would not be getting on the one-year leave. To apply, you needed at least three years of teaching experience, had to be recommended by one's principal, and had to pass the Miller Analogies test. There were study guides for the test and I made good use of them as I wanted to be in this program which would prepare me to get an early childhood supervisory position when I completed it. I was accepted and became a Columbia University student the year I met my husband Miles. I got the MA in Early Childhood Education in 1969. There were no supervisory positions even after I had passed that test and when one became available, I was no longer interested. I was getting married and planned on starting a family.

When the Bernsteins sold the house on Popham Avenue, we moved into one of the beautiful apartments in the building they owned at 1511–1521 Sheridan Avenue. It seemed as though everyone in the family had an apartment there. Aunt Norma and Uncle Willie, who had arrived in New York in 1947, (I also spoke at her funeral); Max's Uncle Phil Dutkowitz and his wife Goldie and their daughter Cookie; Erwin and May; Sam and Phyllis later on; and a few Wengrovers like the Ptaks, and Leah Mazur. Max was generous with fair rent for them. This was a prosperous income producing eight-story, 220-apartment piece of real estate purchased in 1951. It was a desirable neighborhood in the West Bronx, opposite Taft High School, near the Lebanon Hospital, and a stairway distance from the Grand Concourse, the Champs Elysee of the Bronx. Max had an office on the lobby floor of the building where he had an adding machine, kept records of the repairs, and communicated with the on-site superintendent. This is where tenants brought the rent at the beginning of each month. Max would then go to the bank and deposit the checks or cash.

Eventually, Sam and Erwin and their families moved to a poultry farm on Route. 9 near Freehold, NJ in 1953. I frequently visited them and even helped to candle and pack the eggs. I enjoyed being with the kids and actually hung out with all my first cousins once removed (who all assumed I really was their aunt.) They were May's five kids, Joyce, Bruce, Stuart, Robert and Dona; Sam's son, Howard; and Tobi and Phil's kids Paul, Richard, and their twins, Barbara and Sandra. The whole Bernstein family got together for celebrations and special times of the year like their Fourth of July barbecues on the farm. These barbecues were very festive and fun, involving lots of meat eating and dancing Middle Eastern dances with Sam on their large patio. Robert very kindly also reminded me how I sang to him at bedtime when he was four years old. He knows these concerts were very special to him as he remembers not too many other events from that young age.

As I wasn't meeting my intended living on Sheridan Avenue, I decided to move to Manhattan with my friend Judy Basch. Max and Esther felt girls only moved away when they got married, so it was a surprise to them, though they could not forbid it. I was employed as a teacher and earned enough to support myself. My teacher salary was $4000 per year. Judy and I moved to a beautiful apartment at 155 East Thirty-Eighth Street. It was a doorman building, a safe neighborhood, and was accessible to concerts and plays, Shakespeare events in Central Park, and the many museums, which Judy has indicated I introduced her to. When that rent went up to about $250/ month we moved to the Eastmore House on East Seventy-Sixth Street and Second Avenue.

Even though I lived in the city, I was very involved with my brothers and their families. After Sam's wife, Phyllis, died in 1965, Sam was single 'til he married Rena in 1973. During his single days, he and I would go to the Feenjon in the village. Here people danced in the aisles to Middle Eastern music, like Arabic, Hebrew, and Armenian, and we were very willing participants. Occasionally, my roommate Judy and another friend, Linda Grossman, accompanied us and joined in. When Judy and I moved to the city, Sam was our handyman, helping us set up the apartment, hang pictures, and do other repairs. He was always very helpful and giving.

My vision of the world as to what was normal had certainly changed from the one I had from the ages of three to twelve. I had family, friends, and wasn't torn away from people dear to me.

Max succumbed to ileitis and died on August 28, 1969. I had already been dating my future husband Miles, a handsome Jewish lawyer who lived in Jamaica Estates, Queens. We met at a party on December 2, 1968 arranged by one of his friends who actually started dating my friend Judy after that party. Miles came over during Max's *shiva* on Labor Day weekend when I proposed to him! "So when do you want to get married?" I asked. He suggested Christmas vacation, but I offered earlier in the month as I indicated I wanted to have the week of Christmas vacation to set up our apartment. Once again, one of my brothers, this time Erwin, came with an offer. "You can have your wedding on my boat!" Though he actually sold his boat before our wedding, we did get married at his house, at his temple in Lakewood with Rabbi Yedwab as the officiant. On December 6, 1969, I became Mrs. Miles Glantz. But not before I had to take a very unusual test: the Galitzianer test.

A few months after meeting each other, I told Miles about my early life. I don't remember his exact reaction, but he seemed to take it matter-of-factly and calmly. He was familiar with the Holocaust history because some members of his own family had survived Auschwitz, and others had perished. He did tell his family about me and mentioned my ability to speak Yiddish to his mother. So when I met her, she said, "I hear you can speak Yiddish, Gloria. Let's speak a little Yiddish." So we did.

Rose Glantz wanted to be sure her son was not marrying a Galitzianer! (A person from the Galicia region of Poland, reputed—

falsely—to be loan sharks, crooks, and unpleasant people. Their Yiddish was recognizable because of their pronunciation of certain words.) Her mother had stopped at an inn in Galicia overnight and when she opened her suitcase the next day, it was missing all her precious belongings. Her brother had married a Galitzianer woman and the family disliked her intensely. So my future mother-in-law wanted no Galitzianers in the family. I passed the test.

We had had a lovely courtship with dinners, concerts, movies, and family get-togethers. One event stands out as it is definitely a remnant result of my early restricted and difficult life. While I never starved, I was never overfed and always valued every morsel, not wasting anything; I am the poster child of the Clean Plate Club. Our daughter Jordana is aghast that in restaurants where the portions are large and people always go home with doggie bags, I rarely do. I'm also the queen of leftovers, reinventing new ways of serving leftovers or serving them alongside a new side dish or salad so I don't have to throw them out.

So while we were courting, I had a very memorable meal, which Miles and I still laugh about. The lights were dim enough for us to look good but bright enough to be able to read the gold-trimmed, beribboned, four-page menu. A very fine restaurant on Second Avenue in New York City was our choice. It was close to my apartment.

As I perused the menu, I came to a selection called mixed grill with veal, lamb, chicken, Hungarian goulash, and a side of vegetables and potatoes. All of the size five of me had not eaten all day. My stomach was telling me with not-so-subtle noises that I was ravenous. But my past experience with some previous mixed grill items, especially in Japanese restaurants, had taught me that often, each of the listed items appeared as dots on the plate and had never sated my hunger.

"I wonder how the mixed grill will be. Will it be enough for me?"

My boyfriend voiced this concern to the tuxedoed, solicitous waiter.

"Oh, sir, we have some of the New York Giants come here for dinner. And sometimes they can't finish it."

"I'll have the mixed grill."

I mowed down every morsel.

As the waiter cleared the table, he said, "Lady, I wouldn't mind keeping you in clothes. But in food—forget it!"

My boyfriend became my husband anyway.

Sam took over the business of the real estate. One day when Sam was in the office, a black man with a gun entered and demanded the rent money. I think he also took the adding machine. Fortunately, he did not hurt Sam. That incident certainly affected me. A few weeks later, I was waiting for the elevator when a young black father and his little boy about four years old were also waiting. The elevator door opened, and he motioned for me to go in. I wouldn't. He even looked at me and called me on it, "I'm here with my son!" I had stereotyped him; he was black. A black man mugged my brother. This was more than fifty years ago, and I still remember it, ashamed of my behavior. Today, I teach tolerance and acceptance. I give workshops on the subject.

Teaching, growing, living a more normal life in a democratic country. Leaving the life of Gloria Bernstein, and on to my own nest, the Glantz nest.

1. New year's party in basement of Aunt Esther and Uncle Max's house

2. Friends: Gloria, Judy, Linda, Brenda
3. Friends at fiftieth Hunter High School reunion: Linda, Sunny, and Stephanie

4. Sam dancing Middle Eastern dance
5. Sam in his Air Force uniform
6. Max's parents, Sima and David Bernstein
7. Sam, cousin Fishl from Israel (seated), Gloria, Esther (standing)

CITATIONS PART 4—AMERICA (THE BERNSTEINS)

1. https://history.state.gov/milestones/1921-1936/immigration-act (Immigration data)

PART 5

⚜

MY OWN NEST

CHAPTER 1

BEGINNING ANEW

Judy, my roommate on Seventy-Sixth Street, moved out when Miles and I got engaged. We were married on December 6, 1969 in Lakewood, New Jersey. While my youngest brother Erwin offered his boat, he had already sold it by that time so Temple Beth Am in Lakewood was an acceptable substitute venue. It was not a lavish affair because Max had recently died so the family kept it very simple. May was my matron of honor, Miles' best man was Shelly Cohen, his good friend from Scarron Manor on Schroon Lake where they were bus boy and waiter. We had cocktails at May and Erwin's home in Lakewood at 5:00 p.m. and proceeded to the temple for a 7:00 p.m. ceremony. After the ceremony, we ate a gourmet rib steak meal, contributed by Sam, our meat connoisseur. Only close family on both sides were invited. The Morantzs, Ginsbergs, and Shapiros from Montreal rejoiced with us as they had previously promised when I left them. The family rooted to the Przepiorkas, the family I lost, were Esther and her sons, Sam, Phil, and Erwin; and Norma and her children, Roberta and Paul. It was a joyful Saturday night but bittersweet, because Esther and Mendl Przepiorka, my parents, didn't see their little princess as a *callah* (bride). My brothers, Zelig and Yitzchak couldn't hold the chair for their little sister in the *freilach* (happy) circle wedding dance.

To be fair, we invited very few friends.

My wedding gown was quite traditional and suited my petite size 5 figure and my love of lace. Someone recommended a whole-sale outlet in Manhattan's clothing district where they would make a gown to order for each bride-to-be in three weeks. I saw several samples and picked the sleeves of one, the neckline of another, the skirt of another, the fabric of the last. After one week, I was notified my gown was ready to be picked up and instructed to bring $150 cash for payment!

After our wedding, we continued to live on Seventy-Sixth Street for about one and a half years until I became pregnant. We wanted to start a family fairly soon as we were considered an old bride and groom for the 60s and 70s. I had an easy pregnancy but needed to have a forceps delivery when I gave birth to our son. His head was mashed from the forceps and he looked like a little old man, but I nursed him and loved him immediately. We had prepared a crib and changing area for him and some t-shirts and sleeping pajamas from a very popular baby furnishings store called Henry Behr. We were anxious for him to have the proper furnishings and infant clothes. I still remember the hospital pediatrician giving new mother advice. He said, "You can have him sleep in a file drawer and he will thrive, as long as you feed him and love him." And speaking to an inexperienced nursing mother, he added, "Don't worry that he's not getting enough milk. For two-thirds of his life he will be on a diet!" I really needed this encouragement as my mother-in-law kept saying, "How do you know if he's getting enough?" Though I appreciated her concern and later, her help, I thought to myself: If God wanted me to know that he'd have put numbers on my nipples.

Our son Craig Matthew, whose Hebrew name is Mendl Israel, was named after my biological father and Uncle Max, my adopting father. At the time, there were no accurate tests to determine the sex of a child; there were only *Bubbe Moises* (tell-tales), such as if you carry low, it's a boy; and if you carry high, it's a girl. I never measured whether my protruding belly was high or low, but I was fairly certain I would have a boy. I even baked cakes for the *bris* (circumcision done when a boy is eight days old) and had them ready in the freezer!

Max's Uncle, Philip Dutkowitz was the *sandek* (the person who holds the baby during the bris, usually a grandfather). Supposedly the *sandek* passes on his good qualities to the baby. In addition, being chosen for this honor is considered a blessing for long life.

Craig did not have any grandparents who were blessed with a long life. So Uncle Philip had that honor.

http://www.chabad.org/library/article_cdo/aid/144125/jewish/The_One_Who_Holds_the_Baby_The_Sandek.htm (citation) # 1

We picked the name Craig because we didn't want him to have a name that would be altered, such as Jonathan, which could be shortened to John, or Robert to be shortened to Rob or Bob. And Craig went well with *Glantz*. However, another surprising appellation awaited, when, as a youngster, he went to a day camp.

We now needed a larger apartment. We found one in Jamaica Estates, Queens, close to where Miles' mother and sister lived. It was also a short walk from the 179th Street subway station, an easy commute to Miles' job in New York City.

175-27 Wexford Terrace was an unimposing eight story pre-war building with a buzzer and key entry. Once in the lobby, one had a choice of an elevator on the left and on the right to enter the appropriate apartment. There was a non-functioning fireplace, a carpet in the center, and two couches facing each other.

Wexford Terrace was one block off a very busy street called Hillside Avenue. This street was traffic-laden, had a convenient Waldbaum's supermarket, and a Kentucky Fried Chicken, with a little park opposite it. While the little park was handy to have around if one had a baby carriage and wanted to sit down after a walk, the intersection was so busy and congested that my Aunt Esther, my Mom, who had an apartment across the hall from ours, was a bit frightened to cross over to it with her new grandson, Craig, in the carriage. It was convenient to have grandma, a free babysitter, as well as Maria, daughter of the building superintendent who lived on our floor, as a babysitter for a small fee.

Immediately across the street from our apartment building was a new building called The Camelot, which had a large concrete playground on the side with a bench swing and two other children's playground features—a swing and a seesaw—and lots of space for kids to run or ride a tricycle. I spent many hours there at different times of the day, and my children found a few age-appropriate playmates there. But its best feature was the indoor pool in the building, with an outdoor sitting area, which, for a fee, one could use without actually residing in the building. We took full advantage of that. I was grateful it enabled me to swim laps all year round and have a place for our family to relax outside, and swim in the summer.

From my kitchen window of the third-floor apartment, we could see the Mary Lewis Academy, a Catholic high school for girls. Though having a well-behaved group of students nearby was a comfort, the spell was broken one day when, as I was preparing some baby food, I looked out the window and saw an elderly woman being mugged, her pocketbook grabbed as she walked, and the perpetrator quickly disappearing into a waiting car. Suddenly, the barred gates on our windows seemed a necessity.

Most of the time, I felt safe in the neighborhood however. If I walked about two blocks east on my street, I would reach Midland Parkway, an elegant area of Jamaica Estates, Queens. The wide avenue with a grassy center island had many imposing homes, including one owned by Fred Trump, the father of future president Donald Trump.

Many well-designed and maintained apartment buildings he owned also dotted the Jamaica Estates landscape. In the summer, the gorgeous array of color from the flowers on the manicured lawns was a treat from the monotony of the fall greenery. In the winter, the variety of Christmas and holiday decorations brightened the early darkness.

An eight-pound, thirteen-ounce gift in the form of a delicious little girl named Jordana Lynn arrived on April 25, 1973, twenty-five months after her brother. She must have loved the warmth of the womb as she arrived about three weeks after her due date, sufficient time to become round and well-developed! After the initial cry at birth, she was placed on my chest, looked up at me, stopped crying, and had a serene and peaceful look on her face. Even though babies cannot see, the bond was formed. Could I give this little girl, or her brother, away to a relative stranger? I was now a mother. I could not imagine bringing either one of them to a stranger's house without even a parting kiss knowing I would probably never see them again. The courage of my mother, her sacrifice, were beyond my imagination. Elie Wiesel, speaking of hidden children, expressed my thoughts so eloquently: "When exactly did they understand the fathomless strength their parents needed to give up their children to a stranger in order to spare them their own fatal destiny? On the brink of death, their parents pulled themselves away from their children so as to shield them from death." #2 Wiesel, p.150.

Jordana was an early talker and would dance circles around her older brother who was clanging on an old pot drum with a wooden spoon, while singing, "My brother Craig, he's the biggest, he's the best." One might wonder why I didn't name her Esther, after my own mother. I couldn't do that because my adopting mother was also Esther. In the Jewish Ashkenazic tradition, we don't name after a living person. Jordana's Hebrew name is Yocheved Chaya. Yocheved is Moses' mother's name, and Chaya was my beautiful aunt, my mother's sister.

Our apartment was spacious enough for our two young children who had their own rooms and a full bathroom. I kept wishing that we could own our own house, however, the downstairs tenant kept complaining that the children ran around too much and were too noisy. Also, the washer and dryer were in an outdoor area necessitating a coat and boots in the winter just to do laundry, and sometimes several trips as there were only two machines and two dryers for the entire building.

We had some new friends in the area, Pat and Bob and their two little girls, Cara and Shayna; and the Zachos family and their two girls, Terri and Toni. Another couple, the Chusteks, also had small children. We kept in touch with them for a long time after they moved away from the area and even after we moved to Port Washington.

As I look back now, years after moving to the suburbs, my memory is awash with the growth, fulfillment, happiness, the awakenings, and satisfactions of daily life in that third-floor apartment at 175-27 Wexford Terrace. This is where I went from being a newlywed to a mother of two active, healthy youngsters. Here I practiced the art of entertaining, cooking, and baking, and making small dinner parties for our friends. I remember my neighbor, Steve, on the eighth floor, loving my cheesecake so much I would call him if I had any leftovers and tell him, "Steve, meet the elevator. The cheesecake is on its way up."

It was a sweet time in so many different ways.

We had many interesting trips when Miles took his two-week vacation in the summer. Some of these were while still lived at Wexford Terrace and others when we moved to Port Washington. We visited the national parks, Bryce and Zion, which involved long car rides. Every car trip was accompanied by the chorus from our children in the back seat: "Are we there yet?" Jordana recently reminded us of a trip to the White Mountains in New Hampshire. She remembers her dad's shiny suit, her green dress, and the bracelet with little poodles on it she got in the gift shop. A visit to the gift shop was compulsory everywhere we went. We also explored historic American cities such as Washington, Charleston, and Savannah.

Another compulsory stop was a visit to the Visitors Center in every state, especially Virginia, so Craig could pick up brochures for his state report. After these cities, we rested at the beautiful beaches in Hilton Head, South Carolina, where our three families rent a house on the beach every summer. The last trip there was July 22–29, 2017. We already have our reservation for this year, July 7–14.

Both our children have inherited this love of travel and give these experiences to their own children. Jordana has taken Maxwell to California, the girls to Charleston, and arranged family trips to Washington DC, Philadelphia, Baltimore, Savannah, Florida, and Mexico. They are under fourteen!

Craig's children have been to St. Martin, Florida, Mexico, and Hilton Head. I am sure they also have a trip to New Orleans in their future, so Lexi can experience *Mardi Gras*, and learn where her yards of beads originate. Seven-year-old Lexi goes nowhere without beads on! Her five-year-old brother, Judah, loves all those travel adventures.

One of my most memorable trips was The March of the Living (MOL) with Craig. This is an international educational program for people from all over the world to experience Poland and Israel for a fuller understanding of the Holocaust period. Even after this trip and many courses I have taken, I still cannot understand or fathom how civilized people were capable of inventing such cruelty.

During that trip, we saw young people of many nations with their nation's flags, and a sea of blue and white provided by Israeli marchers' flags.

I was moved to compose new words to the Partisan Song traditionally sung in Yiddish, (now Hebrew words too). It is sung at all ceremonies and Holocaust commemorations, and many survivors consider this song their anthem. It represents their victory over death. They are here! My words below and a view of young Israelis on the Auschwitz tracks with their flag.

http://www.dw.com/en/march-of-livin -marks-
holocaust/a-1575086 citation#13
Original words by Hirsh Glik, (Music by Dmitri Pokrass)
These words by Gloria Glantz were written May
2005 on the MOL (March of the Living trip.
https://search.yahoo.com/yhs/search?hspart=pty&hsimp=yhs-
pty_maps&param2=a65a6b7e-9e8f-41ee-92b0-255750562532&par
am3=maps_6.3~US~appfocus29&param4=Bing_
v2-bb8~Chrome~hirsh+glik&param1=20171214&p=hirsh+glik&type=
ma_appfocus29_cr
Citation about H. Glik above

Hirsh Glik was a Cracow carpenter who wrote the Partisan Song in 1943
while he was in the Vilna ghetto. I was safely Maria Kowalczyk's arms.
His Cracow countryman and possibly his mentor, Mordecai Gebirtig,
who also composed many ghetto and freedom songs, died in Partisan
action in the forest in 1944. One of my favorite Gebirtig songs is *Es Brent*
(It is Burning), which I have sung to my children and grandchildren
numerous times. (Citation #1) The Holocaust Chronicle, p.325.

1. We've come together to
remember, understand,
We are a people marching
proudly hand in hand.
Our aching hearts are numb
with distant memory,
The pain and tragedy
that's left as legacy,
And each of us a special
remnant of the past,
Of a religion and a
people born to last!

2. Some are from Cracow,
Lublin, or a shtetl town
You lost your family and your
loved ones never found,
Some were in ghettos, camps,
places no eyes should see,
Filth, illness, danger were
your constant company-
Hunger extreme, a piece of
bread was your best friend,
You hoped to live each day
and make it to war's end.

3. Warsaw was once a city
full of thriving Jews,
Before the ghetto and the
Umschlagalatz were news,

Here brave youth fought to
die with dignity unseen,
Some spent their last breath
in the dark Mila 18!
We won't forget these
heroes of our recent past,
Who showed that Jewish
people could resist at last!

4. We know Treblinka
is a cemetery plot,
We can't imagine the
torment, 'twas there begot.
The jagged edges of the
stones that one can see,
They represent a Jewish
town not meant to be,
The birds and trees, just like
a peaceful picnic ground,
Belie the ghosts and bones
that lie there with no sound.

5. Some of you stood in
dread in Auschwitz-
Birkenau,
We're awed that you survived
it and can't fathom how.
The face of evil is etched
deeply in that place,
It will take many
generations to erase.

But all of us, your kids
and grandkids walking
free,
We pledge a better world
for all humanity.

6. Some of you lived in
woods or hidden
underground.
Chances to run away, be
saved not easily found,
Your perseverance, guts,
and some luck, got you
through
So in this great land you
could start your life anew,
And we are blessed with priceless
joys that can't be bought,
We're free, we're here and
we're the miracles
you've wrought!

7. Why are we here? To
mourn, remember,
celebrate,
Your being with us marks
our victory over hate.
Each child you nurtured,
the successes of your day,
Have shown that we're proud
people and we're here to stay!

Our loved ones, martyrs,
always in our memory,
We'll work together for a
world that is hate-free!

Original "Partisan
Song" (In Yiddish)
*To zog nit keynmol az du
geyst dem letstn veg,
Khotsh himlen blayene
farshteln bloye teg,
*Kumen vet nokh undzer
oysgebenkte sho--
Es vet a poyk ton undzer
trot: MIR ZAYNEN DO!*
*(Sing last two lines twice)
or the English translation:
Never say that there is
only death for you
Though leaden clouds may
be concealing skies of blue,
*Because the hour we have
hungered for is near;
Beneath our tread the earth
shall tremble: we are
here!
*(Sing last two lines twice)

Today Treblinka is a cemetery memorial of 17,000 rocks, small and large, emblazoned with the names of Jewish communities destroyed by the Nazi peril. Wegrow is one of them.

http://www.hoiocaust.cz/en/historv/
concentrationmamps-and-ghettosgtreblinka-3/1

There were many sweet times, and some challenging. Life proceeded and keeps proceeding. A poetic summary of the first thirty-five years of marriage and family is provided by our children at our thirty-fifth anniversary celebration. It follows below:

Craig & Jordana's Thirty-Fifth Anniversary Tribute

This is the tale, the tale of two souls
Who are now a bit wrinkled and a little old.
They started out on different sides of the sea
Who would have known they were meant to be.
Many years in the making and here's how it starts

The path to our celebration of these lovable old
farts.
From a town in Poland did little Gloria come
Through many homes and families
It was a miracle done.
From Poland, to Sweden and then Montreal
But New York City came to be the end all.
In Middle Village do we find our hero Miles,
A skinny boy with long legs and unassuming
smiles
To sisters June & Enid he was the loving big
brother,
Who caught a Yankee baseball, then given away
by his mother.
(Ah, you can just catch another one.)
For Gloria, growing up led to schooling at
Hunter,
Where she made lifelong friends who would
always be there for her.
Teaching and traveling, with many dates in
between,
She wondered "Will I ever be somebody's queen?"
For Miles, there was military school, the army,
NYU,
Summers at Scaroon Manor, with his friends, the
mountain crew.
Law School came next, a *juris doctor* he would be,
Would he meet the woman of his dreams? He'd
have to wait and see.
Then came a party, it was the fateful night,
When Miles spotted Gloria it was love at first
sight.
The party wound down, but he hung around,
All in the hopes that romance would be found.
Movies, museums, dates around town.

Wherever there was one, the other could be
found.
After a year, the question came to light,
Would there ever be a wedding night?
Miles was slow to say the least,
So Gloria said, "When do you want to get mar-
ried?" He was for Christmas, for her that was late,
So she went ahead and set the date.
December 6th, 1969
They vowed to be together 'til the end of time.
It wasn't long before the scamper of little feet,
With Craig then Jordana, the family complete.
A house in the burbs would be in the cards,
Where the kids could have fun, friends and
backyards.
The kids, the temple, working and friends,
Filled their weekdays and their weekends.
Vacations all over the US of A,
There was never a slow or uninteresting day.
The kids went to college, and empty was the nest,
Perhaps now it was time for some much-needed
rest.
Instead they would embark on travels and study,
Enriching themselves so they wouldn't become
fuddy duddy.
(At least not Gloria anyway.)
She is a swimmer, a teacher, a good friend to call,
Known as the town walker to many and all.
A singer, a dancer, a poet extraordinaire,
Her signature trademark—black and silver hair.
He reads every paper, yells at the TV,
A funnier curmudgeon you never will see.
He's a walking encyclopedia, overflowing with
knowledge,
Like that nutty professor we all had in college.

She prefers Mozart,
He likes the Jets;
She threatens to throw out his papers,
He says, "Gloria, quit hockin' me!"
An odd couple from the outside looking in,
But the love they have for each other goes deeper
than skin.
Through good times and bad do they always
endure,
Their love for each other simple and pure.
As your children you've made us the people we
are,
We learned from you always to raise the bar.
We thank you for your love, your understanding
and care,
We think we've turned out a pretty good pair.
So now we come to the end of this tale,
On this, your 35th anniversary, do we all hail.
We all raise our glasses and toast you with heart,
To your life together, a true work of art.

Actually, a very accurate description of their parents with opposing political and personality traits who are, in spite of this, devoted to each other, and yes, they "turned out a pretty good pair."

The Holocaust behind me, or is it? A definite reaction to my early life occurred when Miles' boss, who had relocated the headquarters of his firm to Princeton, New Jersey, told Miles we had to relocate there, too. I reacted with fury! "I like the house! I like the neighborhood! The kids are going to a good school! I'm not moving! I've lived on two continents, in four cities by the time I was twelve!"

"What do you mean your boss would like to move to Princeton? Just because he bought a house there, he moved the company headquarters there!!"

Until then we had agreed on all the big events in our lives: how to act with our kids, how to finance vacations, where to go on vacations, where to settle and buy a house. We even agreed on the furniture we bought!

But I had moved around enough. At that time, I wanted to stay where my friends, family, my heart and my memories were.

Fortunately, it worked out. Ultimately, we didn't move and my husband still kept his job. Now the tables are turned. I want to sell the house and move to a nearby condo. My husband says, "No, this house is where my memories are."

CHAPTER 2

IN CONTROL

Why do I write songs, letters, and poems? It grants me the freedom to be me. After being stifled for the early years of my life—don't speak, don't say this, do this, don't tell, do as I tell you—I can now express fully who I am and what I want to say. Writing is my liberation!

Also, writing is my way of attempting to be worthy of having been rescued. I do a little more, put in more effort; I show others how I care. It's easy to buy a card and sign one's name. I expend a bit more time, making it more personal. (Miles says I could write for Hallmark!) Others can recognize my effort. I still want approval from others and have a desire to look good. I want to be the best Gloria I can be so I will be deserving of having survived. Or do I want to be caring for others because others cared for me?

I also want the freedom to control my life. I want to have a say in what comes next. Thus, I have also become too controlling toward my children. For instance, I know I have tried to convince Craig and his wife Katie to live near me in Port Washington. I have constantly sung its praises on all fronts—schools, JCC programs, good commute to the city, homes available right on my street—even after having been told it was too far for Katie's family to travel from Cape Cod, Massachusetts. My children have explained other understandable reasons, too. Craig has said he doesn't want to live where he grew up. Initially, this shocked me and upset me until he clarified that it was not because this community was a bad place to spend one's childhood. He wanted a different adventure and environment. I probably also give advice when I should stay out of their lives, even though they are usually polite with their criticism when I do.

I survived. I wasn't better than anyone who didn't, just luckier. I have no guilt about it. Nobody died because I lived. But because I did survive, I have to be worthy and deserving of it. So whatever I do—project, workshop, presentation—I spend an inordinate amount of time to make it the best it can be. I have presentations, for example, that I have done for school groups and teachers programs. If I'm doing the same topic for an event at my synagogue for the *Chaverim* (temple group of seniors), most would think of tweaking one or two slides and it's done. Not me. I will spend another twenty-five to thirty hours on it, sometimes adding or making changes even on the morning of the presentation;

For the same reason, I strive to make every minute count. This is definitely a neurosis for me. I don't procrastinate. I don't want to waste time but use each part of my day productively. Here is a typical day for me as a retired sixty-five-year-old woman. Some of the menu and the activities have changed in my seventies, but a full day is what I still expect of myself.

A Day in the Life or Gloria Glantz, the Retired Go-Getter

> 7:00–7:30 rise and shine, wash (rinse face thirty times the Erno Laszlo way)
> 7:45–8:15 breakfast, (a protein and toast)
> 8:15–8:45 read New York Times
> 9:00–10:30 walk about four and a half miles (in dry weather)
> 10:45 Hard-chew snack (celery or cabbage)
> 11:00–12:00 Check, write, and/or answer e-mails, make calls
> 12:00–1:00 Cook or bake as necessary

1:00 Lunch, (salad and protein) NY Times cross-word puzzle
2:00 JCC to swim seventy-two laps (1 mile) (especially if hadn't walked)
4:00 Library - get book club book, write
5:30–7:00 Food shopping, dinner prep, and dinner
7:00–11:00 Read, write, relax with Miles

This was an easy, average day. If I have a workshop to give or take, or to give testimony, a doctor's appointment, a choir rehearsal, or a babysitting gig, things become a bit more rushed. On those days, I might be polishing a presentation or amending a PowerPoint and possibly omitting a workout.

Clearly, I am neurotic about using every minute of my day. Walking is a constant for me—all seasons, weather permitting, and not only for physical health and well-being. I wrote the following piece to attempt to explain the thoughts, ideas, and hopes that whirl about in my psyche as I walk.

I am a walker. Invariably, there are cars with people asking me for directions. About twenty-four years ago when I was on chemo-therapy, a car stopped and asked for directions to the North Shore Animal League, a favorite destination for non-residents of Port Washington. I had been walking, composing my obituary, tears streaming down my cheeks. I directed the driver appropriately, and he looked at me and thanked me. I can just imagine him saying to himself, *I only asked her for directions.*

When I walk, my mind fills and empties. It conjures up, accepts and rejects, regrets and rejoices. It composes and creates, solves, relishes, and remembers.

I walk the walk of an athlete, a woman, a friend, a teacher, a student, a survivor. I walk as a parent, a child, a disciplined older woman with the curiosity and hope of a younger one. Each mile is not only an accomplishment, it is a mission.

Part of the mission of memory is the determination to keep the memory alive. Another part of that mission is to conjure up how many would have lived ordinary or splendid lives. Also, seeing clearly the obligation to preserve the gifts and blessings of my freedom. And lastly, realizing that I must preserve that freedom by being well informed and active in supporting the worthy elements of causes that keep us free.

The mission of forgiveness is a difficult one. And there is no fast-forward to forgiveness. I ask myself: Is it appropriate to forgive those who stole my family's dignity, even before stealing their lives? For those who stood by and let it happen? Each step is a seed of my bitterness, of potentials not realized, people not known. It is the infection I hope to conquer, and one day, to discard and rid myself of forever.

There are steps for the sadness of not being allowed to know Yitzchak and Zelig, my brothers, not having normal sibling rivalry, not having my parents who could rejoice in my accomplishments, not allowing my mother and father to become grandparents, the grandparents my children would love.

There are steps for celebrations of who is left, of who came after, of who survived, of what is joyful in my personal portfolio. I can celebrate the richness of my multi-checkered but rewarding life: a career of making differences in children's lives, being born in a time of hate but giving birth to a time of loving and being loved, raising two children and rejoicing in their successes, of being enriched by the families I have inherited and the one I have created over the years, of understanding and cherishing the heritage I was forced to abandon as a child; my comforts and the many gifts that have come from my labors. Of the music in my life and the songs I've yet to sing.

The miles stretch on endlessly as I add them almost daily. The miles that represent the best of me, still being able to believe in people; not to blame the children for the sins of their fathers and grandfathers; to love; to respect differences; to let go of the hate: to teach tolerance; to embrace new lessons; and to sing new melodies.

The steps I take are as uncountable as the stars, as the names written in the ashes that ascended to the heavens, as uncountable as the cruelties and the degradation perpetrated on my people.

I have been walking for about forty-six years. Yet all the steps of memory, bitterness, sadness, excellence, celebrations, feelings, and fragments have not been exhausted.

Each mile contains endless new steps. New what-ifs, new I-wish-thats, new if-onlies. Also new hopes of tomorrows; a legacy built on history with experience and love. New generations, my grandchildren—a miracle. I was not to have lived past age three or bear children. I was to have gone down in the annals of an extinct race.

New fears that come with the autumn of a life, though it has been a life with promises of springtime and beautiful summers. But also new longings and new wishes; tranquility, and new possibilities.

I am a walker.

Fast forward to August 18, 2017, I had another gut experience. The previous day was humid and ended in a downpour. But that day was sunny and breezy, perfect for my walk. I looked down on the side of a grassy space and noticed four beautiful, saucer-sized mushrooms. Are they poisonous? *The Poisonous Mushroom* was required reading for Germany's young school children. We Jews had been called vermin, virus, bacteria, bogey men, *umgluck* (misfortune), and poisonous mushrooms. My childhood still vivid with me at seventy-eight.

Actually, it is not surprising I had this reaction. Perhaps it was not only the experience of my childhood, but the week before it was easy to be confused about what country we were living in. White supremacists were marching in Charlottesville, Virginia, USA with hateful signs vilifying Jews, blacks, gays, and Muslims. All this with barely tepid criticism from the occupant of the White House, whose mere name makes me tremble with fear. Washington, Lincoln, Truman, Johnson, where are you!

While I have set very high standards for myself, there is no doubt I have also done so for my two children. They never complained about my expectations for them as they were growing up. "Be the best Craig that you can be," I told him, and "Be the best Jordana you can be," I told her. "You don't have to measure yourself or compare yourself to anyone else," I told them both. Our children are a tremendous source of pride for Miles and me. They are ethical and live a life of worth, valuing family, and infusing their children's lives with meaningful and important activities, and supporting them to the extent that they, too, will lead lives of worth and make meaningful choices. For example, on June 25, 2016, Jordana shared information with us about a journey one of her friends and members of her company had taken to Haiti. They had raised money to build homes after the devastating earthquake and decided to sponsor a student with a $35 monthly contribution. This contribution would give them school tuition, healthy meals, and other advantages to help them be successful. Jordana decided this was such a worthy endeavor she would follow suit, sponsoring two students, (with Maxwell's input) a boy and a girl. She continued:

"On a day where I spent enough money on a car that would probably build several homes, I feel good about choosing to help these kids. It's a small financial contribution that is going to change the direction of their lives. And it's a great lesson to my kids about understanding that when we do for those in need, we often get more in return."

In addition, they are both very dedicated to keeping the Sixth Commandment: "Honor thy mother and thy father." I am so touched and so impressed with the many ways in which they show this appreciation. Craig, for example, has a penchant for giving new names to everyone, including his parents, dubbing us "Queen Mum" and "King Pup." This makes him the prince or "The Prince of Surprises." Knowing that Miles watches a lot of TV on a twenty-five-year-old set in our family room, definitely not HD, he delivered a new one at 10:00 p.m. on a stormy night, going after work to buy it, pay for it, and drive it from his Ninth Avenue apartment to our home in Port Washington!

I am also deeply gratified by the way they support each other. Craig surprised Jordana, taking a one-night trip to Atlanta to be there for her fortieth birthday. In turn, Jordana surprised Craig by giving him $5000 after he worked assiduously and succeeded in selling some family property, the proceeds of which were divided by nine family members. He never asked for anything, but she reasoned paying a broker would have cut those proceeds significantly. She concluded, "I didn't do anything to make it happen and I got this nice bit of cash, so I want you to have this." And they've collaborated, too. Jordana participated long distance from Atlanta, contacting about ten of my good friends, for a surprise seventy-first birthday lunch orchestrated by Craig and Katie at a lovely Port Washington restaurant.

They have each contributed to a few of my grey hairs. But now, on the important issues, they bring me pride and joy.

CHAPTER 3

MY CHILDREN AND JUDAISM

The day I *resolved* to write this memoir, January 23, 2016, there was a terrible snow storm, one so severe that the cantor, Claire Franco, of the Community Synagogue where I am a congregant and sing in the choir, had to cancel her youngest daughter's Bat Mitzvah. It was a good day to be at home and begin writing my memoir which I had postponed doing for several years.

A few days later, I notified Craig and Jordana of my intention:

Dear children,

I have begun my 2016 project. It is basically how I went from Gitele Przepiorka to Mother Goose, and the effect that my early life has had on me.

For many years, I felt I am fine now, Holocaust behind me, I'm more than that, I'm not that, etc. But over the last few years, I have begun to realize that the earliest period of my life has profoundly influence the way I behave, the way I act, how I raised my children, what I value, why I work on projects the way I do, why I am so frugal, etc. Also, what I learned from each of my homes—*Matka*, Sweden, Montreal, the Bernstein family, and my own family.

Love you both unconditionally and deeply,
Mom

The following was Jordana's response:

Mom,

This is an incredible undertaking, and I am glad that you are finally moving ahead with it. I know it will not be easy or always pretty, to look back and evaluate the good, bad, and sometimes ugly. As hard as it may be, I do think it will be very important to explore the interfaith relationships (and ultimately the very successful marriages) that Craig and I are both in. I know for our relationship (you and I) this is really a very critical piece, and honestly probably a large part of the resentment and anger that I have felt over the years when it came to the difference in the way you approached those relationships. I know our relationship suffered because I was first down that path. I also think you need to know that those we chose to love was in no way to spite you, or your love of Judaism, but rather because of your experience that I was taught to look at people for who they are and not what they are labeled as, to determine their worth, value, and place in my life. A good person is a good person regardless of race or religion.

I do believe that this book, for everyone involved, will no doubt come with its share of tears and emotion that in the end I think will be cathartic and healing. If I know nothing else, I do believe it will be truly amazing.

Love you,
Jordana

I received Craig's reaction to my writing a book in a phone conversation. There was much more lawyer-like questioning: "Why do you want to write it?" "Who do you want to read it? Only family?" "People don't read books anymore." "If you really want to do it I'm with you."

When Jordana was dating Kevin, and it was clear she intended to marry him, I admit it was a very difficult time for me. She told me he fasted on Yom Kippur, respecting her religion. He also went to services at Emory with her. I knew he was an upright, ethical, and worthwhile person who had all the qualities I wanted my daughter's husband to possess. Except Judaism. I wanted her to marry someone Jewish. Jordana and I visited a psychotherapist to help each of us to deal with this situation. I remember the therapist saying to me, "Gloria, you are very capable and always able to control everything. This is something you can't control, so it is very difficult for you." I have had to learn to be less controlling in the lives of my children.

Even planning Jordana's wedding became problematic. At first, his parents seemed fairly determined to have a priest officiate at the wedding, along with a rabbi. I agreed, but only if it would be a small wedding with just close family and the ceremony would be in a rabbi's study. I felt embarrassed that I, a Holocaust survivor, a reader of Torah and Haftarah in perfect Hebrew, would have a priest at her daughter's wedding. My future son-in-law solved this dilemma for me. He said, "Having a priest at my ceremony means less to me than *not* having one means to my mother-in-law." So we won't have one. A cantor we knew officiated, inserting some readings from the New

Testament. It was a joyful wedding for both families. Kevin is completely accepted and a beloved member of our family and has been so since the first days of their marriage.

Why is Judaism so important to me? Having had my entire family slaughtered simply because they were Jewish has something to do with it. When on a fellowship to Poland and Israel on the Holocaust and Resistance in the summer of 1993, I had the opportunity to study with various well-known Holocaust scholars such as Yehuda Bauer, Michael Berenbaum, and Alan Gilbert. I was aware of Hitler's aim to make the world *Yudenrein* (free of Jews). He had even planned a Museum of an Extinct Race in the Alte-Neue Shul in Czechoslovakia. In addition, there is a 614th commandment for us not to allow Hitler a posthumous victory: Fackenheim's Commandment.

"We are commanded, first to survive as Jews, lest the Jewish people perish. We are commanded, second, to remember in our very guts and bones the martyrs of the Holocaust, lest their memory perish. We are forbidden, thirdly, to deny or despair of God, however much we may have to contend with him or belief in him, lest Judaism perish. We are forbidden, finally, to despair of the world as the place which is to become the kingdom of God lest we make it a meaningless place in which God is dead or irrelevant and everything is permitted." He saw the education of each Jewish child as a victory over forgetting and over darkness.

Service to the ideal of one God, realizing the promise of a triumph over despair, hatred and indifference—this is the 614th commandment the Jewish people, at their best, seek to teach the world. #3 Wolpe, Jewish Week

This knowledge made me so adamant about continuing to have Jewish children, grandchildren, and later descendants. Over thousands of years, others have tried to destroy the Jews. Should we be the ones not to care about our continuity? Truly I don't need a reminder that we should look at people as who they are "rather than what they are labeled as to determine their worth." I treat all people equally and with respect based on their traits not their religion. However, in her e-mail, Jordana made a very valid point when she indicated, "You need to know that those we chose to love was in no way to spite you, or your love of Judaism, but rather because of your experience," that I was taught to look at people for who they are and not what they are labeled as, to determine their worth, value and place in my life.

But I want Jews to exist and thrive, not to be erased from the world's population as was Hitler's plan. Both my children's intermarriages, I feel, constitute a weakened link in that chain of Judaism. Therefore, I have zealously tried to strengthen that link. I have become involved in Temple life, and embrace Jewish customs with tradition and devotion, though not with religiosity.

I recall looking at the *Sefer Zikaron*. (This is a translation from: Kehilat Wegrow; Sefer Zikaron; Community of Wegrow; Memorial book, ed. M. Tamari. Tel Aviv, former residents of Wegrow in Israel, 1961 citation #4 Tamari, M. Sefer Zikaron a book that was co-authored by my cousin Fishl in Israel.) It is a memorial book about my town, Wegrow, and the families who lived there, and died.

The book in my lap whispered names of long ago. It screamed out all the stilled voices. I shuddered at the pictures of the children. There was my stately, light brown-haired aunt Sarah in the sepia print, with her little boy Isaak. This curly-haired boy was a planted bloom that would never emerge with his sweet fragrance and possibility. Perished in Treblinka. Why? He was Jewish.

I turned the yellowish brittle-edged page. Here was Grandma Rachel, tall and slim in a white blouse and dark skirt, with her well coifed *shaitel* (wig). Would anyone believe she had been the breadwinner for their ten children while her husband, my Grandpa Pinchas, studied Torah all day? Killed by a Polish policeman in 1942. Why? She was Jewish.

A hot tear travelled down my cheek.

Another yellowed page. Here was my entire immediate family. My dark-eyed mother; my elegant father in his beautiful suit with white handkerchief in his breast pocket; my handsome brother Zelig, whose face so resembled Craig, his future nephew; my cute, cross-eyed brother Yitzchak with his sad but winsome features. The faces looked out at me as I could almost hear the moans of their frozen throats, their shredded dreams. Perished in Treblinka. Why? They were Jewish.

One more picture faced me. It was me at age fourteen with a caption: "Saved by a Christian. Lives in the United States." This too caused the stone on my heart to feel weighty, ever-present; there was something that gnawed at my innards. Why? I had never even thanked *Matka* properly for saving my life, nor have I ever contacted her or visited her.

It was as though the faces on that page were speaking to me. I imagined hearing their pleas. "Live and remember; do not forget us. You did not take anyone else's life by surviving. You were saved for a purpose." I had always thought I needed to excel to merit my survival. "I survived, so I better deserve it," was my thinking. Perhaps I no longer need to set impossible standards. I was actually awakening to a new task ahead. As I perused the faces on that yellowing page, I became aware that I lived to preserve and cherish their memory, to remember their unfinished songs. Perhaps even to sing them. They would have wanted me to live and do the things I was doing. To live a life that would have made them proud. I had to work to fight malice and prejudice. And very importantly, I had to find a way to show gratitude for being rescued by Marianna Kowalczyk, the uneducated but wise Catholic woman who allowed me to survive the Nazis and live to become a citizen of this great nation, the United States.

When I perused these pages, my chest was not totally unburdened of the sleek, hard stone which had lain there. It was still there. How could I lighten its burden?

Almost every time I give testimony, I am asked the same question: Did you ever go back and see Marianna Kowalczyk? And each time I give the same excuse: I was never permitted to do so. Now I am grown up. I don't need permission. She is gone, but how can I make her memory live on? This question has gnawed at me for many years. How can I honor her for her bravery and kindness? Eventually I found a way.

I also found a way to honor the family I lost as well as the Jewish heritage. I was confirmed at my synagogue in May 1991 at age fifty-two, considerably older than the typical confirmand. A portion of my speech follows.

> It's a long trip from Mt. Sinai to Port Washington. Yet we have all symbolically taken that trip. Today we celebrate, *Shavuot, zman matan torateynu*, the season of the giving of our Torah. The giving of the Torah can be placed historically at a specific time, in a specific place. It can be commemorated. Significantly, the holiday is not referred to as the season of the receiving of the Torah. For the act of receiving can take place anytime, anywhere. It is being given to us continually, and forever. I was there because I am here. And so were you. We received it individually, each of us taking responsibility and collectively as a people. In Deuteronomy, God said, "I make the covenant not only with you alone, but with those that stand here, and with him that is not here this day" (Deuteronomy 29-15). Insurance that future generation would be part of this unique spiritual experience. #4
> http://biblehub.com/deuteronomy/29-15.htm (source)
> We are called the chosen people. Chosen because we were given the commandments and a covenant with God. But we are also a "choosing" people. We agreed to accept the covenant and the responsibilities implied therein. "Na'ase v'nish-mah." (Exodus 24: 7) the Israelites responded "We will do and we will listen." #5
> Tonight I, too, feel myself to be both a chosen and a choosing person. Clearly, I Am Israel

so I fit this category inherently. But also, I was one of the far too few chosen to be plucked out of the fires of hell to pass this covenant on to my children and my children's children. And this evening, I confirm choosing to do so.

Far am I from the time when, as a four-year-old kneeling in front of the Virgin Mary, I feared for my life. As I stand in front of this ark and its awesome treasure today, I celebrate life. Where I once could survive only by hiding my Judaism, I can now openly study it, celebrate it, and cherish it. In this month of Sivan, the month that celebrates abundance, renewal, God's goodness, and the gift of Torah, I too, celebrate my many gifts. The joy of family, the blessings of health, the warmth of friendship, and the beauty of my heritage. Indeed, I feel quite wealthy.

And I share my love of Judaism, our history, with the next generation.

February 12, 2004, the birth day of my first grandchild Maxwell was a time of joy and celebration. The mere fact that I have lived to be old enough to be a grandmother, a right never granted to my parents and aunts and uncles, has led me to write to him and about him. *Yiddishkeit* (Jewish identity/connection) is so important to me, and I hope it will be to my descendants.

Happiness, I know, can come in the form of a very small package. A check for millions, a lottery winning can come in a small package. It can give me many baubles, homes, vacations, and other luxuries. But it will not make me feel victorious. It will not sustain me during emotionally trying times. It will not bring me life in the hereafter. Though I would not refuse it, it can easily be lost, and sometimes even be the root of evil.

A beautiful large diamond can come in a small package. It can impress people. It will sparkle on my finger or on a chain around my neck. It is a thing of beauty, but it will not be a source of wonder at daily changes and yearly accomplishments. It will not be a source of my pride or a means of perpetuating memories from long ago. It will not provide me with any hope or anticipation of an exciting future.

So it is no wonder that the glowing happiness I know comes in the form of miniature perfection. It is alive. Physically, that life is tiny, helpless, and dependent. It cries out for attention, food, comforting, and affection. Yet it is perfectly formed. An almost perfect circle of a head, still pulsating, proportionally too big for its body; a few wisps of brown hair not yet ready for a comb or brush; a face capable of a wrinkled brow or a serious look of contentment, of responding to the sound of the human voice at two weeks, and capable of so many more expressions as the weeks go by; rounded, ample cheeks; large, deep blue pupils that overpower the size of the eyes under, as yet, barely distinguishable eyebrows; the lips of his mother, a full bow-shaped upper lip, and a full, shining lower one; lips capable of housing a long perfect thumb with a functioning knuckle; hands that are perfectly shaped with five, long piano fingers, with little creases on the knuckles, and rounded nails that look manicured though they already need to be filed. The skin is still a little flaky in spots but whipped-creamy soft and smooth; skin color lucent and luscious.

So how can this little package that needs so much attention give me so much happiness?

He helps me turn away from my everyday concerns and obligations, from the mundane "I have to do this," "I need to go there," "I should . . ." to each new expression, each small achievement such as just looking around in his crib at two weeks of age for a half hour without crying; to the hopes and prayers I have for his future; to what he represents for me. The miracle of his being here at all, the miracle that his mother is here at all, the uncanny sense of victory for me of being here to enjoy grandmother-hood, when others have wanted it to be otherwise, namely for me to have died by age three.

Because his life represents all the wonderful opposites of the cousins I had and their cruelly abbreviated childhood, or even the childhood I had that I know and am grateful that he won't have.

He is not merely a beautiful, adorable piece of protoplasm, but actually holds a bit of me, a bit of his great grandparents inside of him. His great grandmother had a beautiful voice, his grandmother, mother, and father also sing. I contemplate the joy of his having music in his life. The guitars adorn the study walls, the piano graces the living room, and his long fingers and large hands look very promising. May he always have something to sing about.

The two dogs (then, now one dog) in his house lick him, guard his house, and protect him. Long ago, dogs mauled Jewish children on command.

My hopes:

- That his parents and family be with him for a long, long time;
- That he grows to appreciate his mingled roots, but also cherishes and practices his Jewish heritage;
- That he has the serenity in his life as his Hebrew name, *Menachem*, connotes, and lives in a world where peace and serenity also prevail;
- That his middle Hebrew name, *Yitzchak*, whose root means "to laugh" will inform his life, but that Isaac's familial importance will underscore his importance and value to humankind;
- That he always knows the history of his family and allows his heritage to sustain him in times of need.

Each day this miniature miracle will change needs and abilities. Though there will be times of upset, dissatisfaction, perhaps rebellion, there will be many more of delight. He has the potentials that will be sources of *naches* (pride) for me.

There is no greater gift than a grandchild who gives me remembrance, a feeling of victory, a measure of continuity, and the recognition of the importance of each small step.

So be a little Yiddish *kind*, (Jewish child) Maxwell. Don't let it disappear. As I look into your eyes, the blue of oceans there I see. The blue of skies that held the days of happiness, of truth, of faith, of heritage. I see the sparkling lights of knowledge, study, and history. But there are also the sparks of furious fires that extinguished those lights and imperiled the rich culture. I see your smile that lights the world, a world you'll brighten with your trust, your innocence, and your truth. And when your innocence is gone, I hope you'll strive to keep the values and the love and acceptance that you have been taught, and of which you are a product.

You'll know your grandma's story and the story of her parents, your great grandparents, great aunts, and great uncles. And maybe, the more you know, the more you'll want to know and learn. And when you are a father, perhaps the tears will trickle down your face when you hear a Yiddish song or sing one to your child just as they flowed down your grandma's cheeks when she sang them to you.

And you won't let the *Yiddishkeit* disappear. *Kein Yihi ratzon.* May it be God's will.

Love from Grandma.

Wish fulfillment sometimes has a way of peeking through. On our 2016 vacation in Hilton Head, I was practicing prayers and Torah reading with Maxwell for his upcoming Bar Mitzvah! This memorable event took place on February 11, 2017.

Though I had some reservations early in their marriage about how much Judaism was prevalent in Jordana's home, I am now deeply grateful that the children are being educated in Hebrew school and our son-in-law Kevin is fully comfortable with Jewish rituals and education. I even thanked him and his family at Emerson and Kenzie's baby namings at the Community Synagogue for allowing them to become *Esther Bracha* and *Zahava Rachel.*

When Craig and Katie became engaged, I experienced a second upset about my child's interfaith marriage, though, again, not about the person he chose to marry. He had been dating a Jewish woman for almost three years in hopes she would be his bride. But over time, he and many of his friends realized that he himself had changed in a way that made him a different Craig, not the one they knew and loved, all to accommodate her wishes. She was a lovely woman, but not the right person for him. They broke up.

But Katie had all the attributes we hoped our son would find in his bride except Judaism. They handled the issue in their own way, taking a six-week course at the JCC (Jewish Community Center) in New York City for couples in interfaith relationships. In this course, they had the opportunity to flesh out their choices on how they would address their differences of faith.

Jewish tradition allows a special ceremony called an *aufruf* to be held for the groom a few weeks before the wedding, for the couple to be blessed in the synagogue during a *Shabbat* (Friday night) service, and for the groom to be called up to the Torah for an *aliyah* (an honor). Although we belong to a reform congregation, our rabbi told us he would not be able to perform this ceremony for them as one partner was not Jewish. He said he would bless them after their marriage, not before. (And he did so). I was not going to let my disappointment cheat my children of this significant event and decided that I would have an *aufruf* in our home for them. Below is the description of some proceedings of the night of Friday September 26, 2008.

Katie and Craig,

All good things come to those who *walk*! So one day on my walk, I got this idea of having a special evening for you. I did a bit of rationalizing to convince myself I could do it. For example:

- Prayer services have been and can be conducted in the home.
- I can read Hebrew and lead a service if I had to.
- I don't have a Torah at home but I do have a Tanakh, the Hebrew Bible, which contains the Torah, the Five Books of Moses, within it.
- Maybe Rabbi/Cantor Yaron can officiate.
- It's extra work, but thankfully there's Ayhan's Mediterranean Market! And I really want to do this.

All this has come to pass. We are fortunate indeed to have rabbi/cantor and friend Jacob Yaron with us. And he has provided us with a Torah, so we don't have to use my books.

But I want to speak about the books for a moment. Katie, look at the name in the book. It is not my present name. It says Gloria Morantz, a name I relinquished about fifty-seven years ago. Nevertheless, I have very special memories of the time I had that name. I was on the threshold of a new beginning.

Katie and Craig, you, too, are on the threshold of a new beginning. And you, Katie will be acquiring a new name. We know you will have many wonderful memories associated with your present name, and we hope and pray this evening will be one of them. A time when a small and dedicated congregation, some of whom won't be at your wedding, joyfully and enthusiastically met to bless you and wish you well. And when the sheen of youth has faded, and both of you become a bit frayed and discolored with age as these books are, you will still savor this memory as you cherish each other. (At least for fifty-seven years.)

To help you hold on to the memory, I would like to give you a copy of this evening's service, which includes all the blessings and prayers for you and the names of everyone here and their individual wishes for you.

Since we do have a Torah here, Craig will now chant his Bar Mitzvah portion, and the appropriate blessings before and after the reading. So he got his *aliyah* (an honor for a blessing before Torah reading) at his *aufruf* on a quiet street in Eastern Crest, not at the impressive temple in Sands Point!

Our living room on that September evening was a Tivoli Garden, lit up by twinkling eyes and sparkling smiles!

Katie and I enjoyed a warm relationship right from the beginning. Even before they were married, we had a museum date at MOMA and then lunch at a nice restaurant nearby. We talked about the museum and the exhibit and I learned a lot from her as she is knowledgeable and gifted in art. We shared some of our experiences, and spoke of her family and her love for Craig. I was so inspired by her psychological astuteness and her emotional, charismatic and free-flowing conversation. She was an attentive listener so interested in our family and my early life experiences. She was genuine and a pleasure to be with.

As time went on, she made an effort to participate in some of the Jewish holidays and traditions. She came to our synagogue on *Rosh Hashanah* and *Yom Kippur* with Craig. She shared in our Seder, even making wonderful Passover macaroons. More recently, she made a Seder in her own apartment, with her mother's help, inviting ten people. She made a big festival in their apartment for *Chanukah*, with decorations and menorah lighting.

I truly appreciate all these efforts, and somehow continued to wish she would continue to include more Judaism while downplaying her own religion. I was made aware of my insensitivity to her. "Why don't you ever say 'Merry Christmas' to me, Gloria?" Of course, it was my own unrealistic wishful thinking that if I didn't say it, it wouldn't be there. I now feel I have to be careful to include that greeting to her and members of her family, and sometimes a little gift to mark the occasion. I am, of course, very happy to do that.

Now I realize I was both ignorant and in denial of Katie's love of her family's traditions, especially her grandma's Christmas celebrations. I also was unaware that Craig and Katie had made a basic agreement after taking the six-week course at the JCC in Manhattan— their children would be raised as Jews. And they would fully celebrate Christmas and Easter as secular holidays. Christmas story books can be found in the children's bookcase along with Jewish holiday books. And they have agreed on a full-size Christmas tree in their home, with unique, non-religious ornaments.

In my heart I wish I could be more comfortable when I see that tree. On the other hand, I am grateful for Katie's family's acceptance and appreciation of our son. And I experience so much joy when I see the depth and power of Craig and Katie's love and support for each other which they exhibit in so many ways. They celebrate special occasions in each other's lives in unique manners. One example follows: Craig enters one of their favorite local eateries on Twenty-Third Street and Ninth Avenue, where there are pictures of famous actors and actresses who have eaten there. Among them is a picture of him (one of his head shots from his attempt at an acting career) which Katie had asked the owner to hang up for one of his birthdays! And Katie opens a huge gift box on her fortieth birthday. In it she finds a very small, sensational gift: two airplane tickets to Paris!

Yes, just as Jordana indicated about herself, I, too, value all people regardless of their faith if they are good people. Below is a letter referring to my colleague, Lorrie, a devoted Catholic. She and I had a beautiful relationship when we taught ESL together at Shelter Rock School. I called her the Long Island Mother Theresa because of her compassion and kindness toward those less fortunate. I considered her a part of our family. When she died, I wrote a letter to her children and granddaughter. Excerpts follow below:

> I will always remember her as the consummate teacher, not only to children, but also for adults. I remember how she individualized instruction, readers, and materials so that they would have the optimum effect on each particular student. She was always concerned about the emotional as well as the academic issues that related to each student. She was willing to give up lunchtime, prep time, after school time to meet those needs, and to help not only the children, but also their parents.
>
> She taught *me* how to be less timid, more self-promoting, to laugh more, to appreciate the struggle to get the best results and get the feeling that the struggle was worthwhile. She taught me to appreciate my own abilities by making me feel tall in her presence (even though we were about the same height). She taught me the ropes at Shelter Rock, which people to humor and which to avoid. We shared so many interests and feelings about ethics, humanity, teaching, and traveling. She delighted me with her humor, her sense of joyfulness, and her cleverness. After getting John's next-to-last e-mail about her no longer wanting visitors, I said to myself, "I wish I could relive my worst day at Shelter Rock with Lorrie." The two of us never had bad days with each other or because of each other. Each day was laced with support, trust, and a common goal.
>
> I was both honored and refreshed by her friendship. Her passing has left a huge hole in my life. Some people never have someone like

Lorrie in their lives. We were blessed by having her though for much too short a time.

It was a privilege for me to be a part of the Longobucco family for so long. Miles and I wish you all the best in all of your future undertakings and a bright and peaceful world for you, Sophia.

Please don't forget us.

Love,
Gloria

CHAPTER 4

My Teaching Career

My teaching experience can be divided into pre- and post-retirement segments. Since I was always interested in languages and had polyglot experiences with several, I naturally gravitated to teaching ESL (English as a Second Language), now called ENL (English as a New Language). Because of a serendipitous discussion with my fellow chorister, Pat Schanzer at a choir rehearsal, I was informed that there was an opening for a teacher assistant in the Manhasset Junior High School with an ESL teacher named Connie Frank. (Pat was the Coordinator of Special Services in the Manhasset School District.) Hooray! A foot in the door into a terrific school district only about twenty minutes from home! I started in September, 1985 in time for a little extra cash for Jordana's upcoming Bat Mitzvah the following April! I loved working with Connie and I loved working with the students. Connie was also happy with me; she said she finally had someone in the classroom who could spell!

Since I had majored in English and had taken several graduate English courses at Hunter College, I needed very few credits to get the ESL certification. A few methods courses during summer session at CW Post, and I had the certification. In the meantime, the Shelter Rock Elementary School in Manhasset was experiencing a rise in the ESL student enrollment, and a teaching position became available there. After a successful interview with the Principal, Richard Koebele, that position was mine.

This was a dream job: small groups of students for one to three hours depending on their English ability, no discipline problems, hardworking kids, grateful parents, an understanding principal, and an able and precious colleague named Lorrie Longo. I taught students in small groups from grades one through six. Since the social studies curriculum included World War II, I was able to include some Holocaust material. With the cooperation of the sixth grade staff and Mr. Koebele, I was allowed to give testimony to each class and the students were asked to write their comments and ask one question which were passed on to me. I returned on another day and answered each person's question. The teachers told me their students' writing gained intensity and depth. In the ESL class, they wrote diaries of a child in hiding, or essays on what they would take with them if they had to leave their homes. They expressed appreciation of their families after they heard my presentations.

One of the highlights of the year was the ESL luncheon held in January or when convenient. The students prepared reports or short presentations about their countries, or the holidays they celebrated with their families. The more advanced students tackled more complex subjects we might have studied. One year, we did a project on whales and even adopted a whale! They wrote about a whale of their choice with scientific information and illustrations. Another year, after some construction had been done at the school, we invited the architect to explain blueprints and certain construction facts. Some of the students used computers to build a house of their own or speak about unusual houses such as igloos and tepees. After the presentations, we were treated to a sumptuous luncheon prepared by the parents. The day ended with a talent show in the auditorium. The students might play an instrument, dances dressed in native garb, or sing a song. Any classes that were free at that time were invited to see the show. A very full and satisfying day for students and teachers alike!

I loved my job but at age sixty-two wanted a little more free time. I retired in June of 2001.

My free time didn't remain free very long. After my 1993 Holocaust and Jewish resistance summer trip to Poland and Israel, I was compelled to learn more and teach more. I read more than forty books and began developing Holocaust workshops for teachers with an emphasis on tolerance and acceptance of people different from us. To this day, when speaking to groups in workshops, I try to include the phrase, "Our similarities unite us, and our differences enrich us."

My experience has brought this to the forefront of my life's work. The recognition that the Holocaust started with shunning others because of their differences and demeaning them to the point where they were no longer people, but vermin to be exterminated.

I am gratified beyond words when I hear students respond to my teaching as indicated below when I received the Outstanding Educator award from the Anne Frank Center. However, before I mention those students, I want to present my son Craig's words upon my retirement. When I retired from the Shelter Rock School in June of 2001, he came from San Francisco where he worked for the law firm Morrison and Foerster. He lauded his mother's teaching ability at her retirement party.

June 5, 2001

When I started to think about what I would say tonight, I didn't know where to begin. One of the teachers being honored, Gloria Glantz, my mom, has had a teaching career that has spanned four decades and has touched the lives of hundreds upon hundreds of school children. While my mom has probably stepped foot in her classroom well over a thousand times, I but only stepped foot in her classroom perhaps five or six times. Even though I obviously know and love a lot about my mom, I was afraid that I didn't have enough firsthand experience seeing Gloria Glantz, the schoolteacher, actually do the job that she is tonight renting from.

But as soon as I started to really think about it, I realized that, in actuality, I was probably the most qualified person at this celebration to say a few words about my mom's teaching career. While most of my mom's students only had the benefit of one school year with my mom, I have great fortune to have received over thirty years of her teaching. And, luckily, I have the great fortune to continue to be my mom's student for many years to come even after her retirement from Shelter Rock. I think it's safe to say that I am, in fact, Gloria Glantz's oldest pupil. And as I look back upon my life, it doesn't take long for me to realize that my mom is, and will always be, the greatest teacher I have ever had.

So, what has Gloria Glantz, the teacher, taught me? She has taught me about the most important thing in life. She's taught me about: love, care, honesty, patience, free-thinking, tolerance, strength, courage, and respect for others; She has taught me the value of hard work, doing your best. She has taught me that, by sharing yourself with others, you can bring the best out of those with whom you have shared. She has taught me the importance of soul. Some of these values she conveyed through her words. Others she has taught me by her example. Either way, my mom has taught me everything out there that is worth learning. And I know that she's done the same for my dad, Miles, and my sister, Jordana.

And even though I didn't actually sit and watch my mom teach a class more than a couple of times, I know from reading the many letters from students and other teachers that my mom has had an equal impact on those outside of our family. And I know from watching her tireless work ethic and her ever-present desire to come up with new and exciting ideas for lesson plans and activities that these qualities boiled over into her classroom and cultivated an ideal atmosphere for learning. Because I know my mom, I know that she threw herself into everything she did and poured her heart and soul on to every student every day of her teaching career.

So, Mom, I know I speak for dad and Jordana when I say thank you for teaching us everything out there worth learning. And I'm sure I speak for many of your colleagues and the children you've taught over the years owe you the same thanks as well. Congratulations on your retirement.

After his speech many guests suddenly offered daughters, sisters, and nieces for him to date!

On June 12, 2002, I was the recipient of the Outstanding Teacher Award from The Anne Frank Center, which focuses on teaching civil and human rights to create the kind and fair world Anne dreamed about. Some excerpts from my speech at that event follow:

"We often exhort children, 'listen to your parents'. But we, the adults, cannot forget to listen to the voices of the children. It is the voices of the children that have inspired me to do the work I do. Through their feedback to me, they have bared their beautiful souls and I like what I see. They have validated my teaching and compelled me to continue promoting the ideals of tolerance and acceptance."

I hope for four outcomes in teaching these ideals:

1. Those children will stand up against bigotry and prejudice.
2. That they will foster understanding and respect for each other.
3. That they will nurture worthwhile values.
4. That they will recognize true heroism and choose worthy heroes.

Here are a few examples of feedback from my students, and what their words say to me:

- Roxanne: "One thing you said I will never forget, "When you have a chance to help someone, even if it is the tiniest bit of help, take it. Not for money or praise, but so that one more soul will be helped."

- Valerie: "The most important thing that I will mostly remember from this presentation is that kindness and love are the strongest tools in life." (This says to me, "Teach about worthy values.")
- Steven: "You taught me to be grateful for my family and everything I have, and to respect and treat people the way I'd like to be treated." (This says to me: teach social responsibility and acceptance.)
- Adam: "If I were to have a hero, it would be someone who would have made a difference in my life and Michael Jordan hasn't. Neither does any actor or rock and roll band. My hero would be Jennifer, my tutor. She made me from a troubled student into a pretty good one."

These sentiments, repeated in different ways hundreds of times, have encouraged me, enlightened me, validated my work, and have imbued me with the zeal to do the work that is the mission of the Anne Frank Center.

My second teaching career began at various school districts even before my retirement. My involvement with the Holocaust Memorial and Tolerance Center began more than twenty years ago when I started giving my testimony and presenting short workshops I had developed for teachers and students. Some of the topics were the Berlin Olympics, Children in the Holocaust, Holocaust Heroes, and Resistance. But it was not only for giving testimony and workshops. I was also continuing my own Holocaust education through the interesting and inspiring workshops given by the capable educators like Beth Lilach and Tracy Garrison-Feinberg.

One of the most useful perks of volunteering at the HMTC was being part of a writing workshop for survivors given in 2003–2004 by a published poet, Veronica Golos, and her able assistant Bonnie Marcus. Our generous librarian and founding member, Marcia

Posner, funded it. It was here some of us shared our stories of survival and critiqued each other's writing. One day, Annie Bleiberg, a participating survivor, brought a cake she had baked to share with us. As she cut the cake, the blue numbers on her arm were visible. On Aril 27, 2004, I was moved to write a poem about her.

Our Annie

The oven is ready. You put the cake in.
There were other ovens. They were for you.
You wanted to live.
"If only they'd let us work," you said.
You blended the flour, the eggs, and the milk.
They blended the young and the old, from Poland, from Greece,
From Italy, from France.
You beat the eggs,
They beat you, little Jewess, your friends, your family.
The cake will rise.
Their ashes rose, not yours
So many things to do, so many things to see, you said,
You jumped, jumped with hope, into the unknown.
Prepare the doily, the beautiful cake plate,
So it looks pretty, like your face
Washed in your tea stained cup,
So justly shared with your *goils,* (girls)
As we taste your cake this day.
Look pretty, so you won't look ill,
So you will please dear Uncle Mengele
So you will live another day.
To bake another cake, so light and tasty

Drop by drop, by teaspoons, the vanilla, a beau-
tiful scent.
By carloads, one by one, they went to the ovens,
The young, the teens, the children, the rabbis,
The doctors, the students, the beautiful people,
The awful stench
But you have no time to write about ovens, it
hoits (hurts) you say,
You laugh and teach, and act, and love,
And bake and serve and bubble.
And share your soaring spirit.
You are our Annie,
Of the rising voice,
The crooked smile,
Of the shining eyes,
The indomitable spirit
The Annie of the tea-washed face,
The *eyshet Chail*, woman of valor with a vanilla
scent,
Pink cheeks and lips, blue numbers on your arm
That deftly cuts and shares the bit of sweetness
of *your* oven

When videoconferencing became available, my horizons
expanded to various national and international audiences. I was compelled to do this after my trip to Poland and Israel. I felt the stories
and history must be told. I was no longer "hidden." I was using my
experience to promote acceptance and tolerance. I was paying back
for all the good fortune I had experienced. Perhaps I was experiencing the high that comes with doing something successfully, being the
best Gloria I could be, and therefore deserving of my survival.

I recently was interviewed for a documentary on PBS which
featured the Holocaust Memorial and Tolerance Center of Nassau
County. I was asked about any specific interaction with students that
I feel is memorable. I mentioned the two incidents below.

After describing the incident of the soldiers coming in the middle of the night with flashlights and me having to prove I was not Jewish by saying my prayers to the Blessed Mother, Mary, I asked the students if they thought I had fooled the soldiers by my polished prayer reciting and convinced them I was Christian. Almost all of them said I had fooled the soldiers. One little girl raised her hand and said, "No, I don't think you fooled them." I further pushed for her explanation why they had not taken me away, but let me live. And she offered, "Perhaps they were benevolent." She got it. There were benevolent people, even Germans.

Another teaching moment that has influenced the way I usually end my testimony each time I speak was given to me by one of my sixth grade ESL students at Shelter Rock School in Manhasset. There was a question and answer time after my speech. Carlos asked, "If you could speak to your real mother and father for three minutes, what would you say to them?" I now respond to that question each time I give testimony. I am forever grateful to Carlos, who has allowed me the right and the opportunity to address my family in an honest and cathartic way. I had never thought of speaking to my parents before.

Just as a student taught me to "speak" my feelings to the family I lost, I was given another opportunity, this time to address my mother specifically. It was at a program with the Long Island Youth Orchestra at CW Post College in Brookville, New York, about ten years ago. The orchestra conductor had taken a group of young musicians to perform at Auschwitz. They performed the theme from *Schindler's List*. It was a beastly hot day, without a trace of a breeze. This was a solemn event so applause was unsuitable. However, shortly after the end of the piece, the leaves started to rustle noticeably due to the arrival of a strong welcome breeze. The musicians felt that the wind was nature's way of acknowledging that life, not evil, had triumphed here. This profound experience inspired the conductor to offer a musical tribute to victims and survivors of the Holocaust.

My contribution was in the form of a poem, which I introduced with these comments:

"My remembrance of my mother physically is limited to her head and her dark, luxurious hair swept away from her face; her inky, deep-set eyes, which today are repeated in our son's face; and the visible mole above her lip on the right side of her face, reflected on my right cheek. The one experiential aspect of my mother that I remember and cherish, because it has remained with me in my love of music and my own soprano voice, is her singing to me at bedtime each night. Ergo, this poem."

What Song Did You Sing, Mother?

What song did you sing, mother,
When you left me behind?
When you walked with my brothers
Driven, by the beating whip.
As you hung your pajamas on the hook,
Did your thoughts wander off to your Gitele at all?
Did the smallest hope that she would go on,
Not perish, but live,
Mitigate some of that brutish hell?
Did you scratch the wall with your gentle fingers?
Till your blood oozed out?
Did you comfort your sons, Zelig and Yitzchak?
Chant Kaddish in advance, for yourself, and for them?
Ai-lu-lu, you sang
to one child, to all children,
to a roomful, to a people
Never to wake from this eternal sleep.
Your voice could soften any heart.
Your song could soothe a grieving breast.
But not then…not ever after.
Did your tears erase your voice

As gas silently seeped into the shower room,
Assaulted your body, clamped-shut your throat.
No more melodies to the children of Israel.
Your black upsweep, turned white, now swept up
Soft as your voice once was, floating as your
image floats,
Through the poisoned clouds of remnants of a
people,
Cleansed by the memory of your sweet melody.

The realization came to me. I had never had a chance to mourn for my mother or anyone I had lost. And my writings to her and about her were really serving a multifold purpose—a celebration of her heroism, an expression of gratitude for giving me life twice, and most importantly, a guarantee of her memory, so she would not suffer a second death. In total, they are a form of *Kaddish*, (a Jewish prayer for the dead) my own personal *Kaddish*, which I had never been allowed to express at the appropriate time.

CHAPTER 5

LOOKING BACK, WRITING

A Sliver of Your Life (The Names I Had)

Mother Goose evokes the innocence of childhood, the lilt of rhymes easily committed to memory by many American children. So far from my childhood in every way.

When our son was born, we wanted to give him a name that wouldn't be shortened. We didn't want a Richard to become Rick or a Joseph to become Joe. So we named him Craig, confident that he would be called Craig and no other name.

We never expected that when we sent him to a local summer day camp at age six, he would come home with an altogether different name. In a children's game of ball, he was encouraged by his counselor to run. *"Go, Goose, go!"* the counselor shouted, referring to Goose Gossage, a popular Yankee ball player at that time. That bit of encouragement was a lot more significant than merely succeeding in a childhood game. The name Goose is what my son inherited, and is still called by some of his high school, college, and law school friends even today. By default and logic, I became Mother Goose. So far from my unrhymed and unpredictable childhood in every way.

What is in a name? A sliver of your life.

A whole life's journey led to Mother Goose, and it certainly would surprise people to learn that she started as Gitl Przepiorka, or Gitele, or Chane Gitl.

I don't know after whom I was named, but it must have been someone good, for "git" or "gut" depending what part of Poland you came from, means good. Life then (the first three years of my life) was the meaning of my name. It was family, mother's beautiful voice, the smell of leather on my father's hands. It was hiding under the bed so my big brothers could look for me in a game of hide and seek. It was loving and being loved. Then it was being left. Przepiorka means little bird. That too was suitable, for I was free and there was singing. Soon the bird had to fly away, not only for the winter, but for all seasons.

Gucia Chanushia, Kowalczyk was a strange name, not only in its sound. It was a Polish version of my birth name, without a trace of the dangerous Yiddish. Also, it was paired with a new and foreign last name, Kowalczyk. Everything about that time was strange, unknown, and unfamiliar. No more Shabbat or Chanukah. Now there was Christmas, prayers to *Matka* Boska, pictures of a bleeding man on a cross. Just who was I now? I was no longer free as a Przepiorka but hidden and restricted. It was a time of missing, pining, and praying. A time of cringing, crying, forgetting, pretending. And then, once again, a time for loving, a time for leaving, and a time for letting go.

Then came Guta, same as the original meaning of good, but it has a guttural sound, a cold and institutional feeling. An orphanage, long tables, smelly, bony herring. Crowns of candles at Christmas; my first foreign language, of which only one Swedish phrase "*tack sa mycket*" (thank you very much) remains. Long, lonely nights and short, fleeting days in the Land of the Midnight Sun. Again, leaving to I don't know where on a ship.

Gloria sounds Latin, American, glorious. *Gloria in Exceslis Deo*, the irony of the source of this, the religion that helped me to survive. Still a life with strangers. But a familiar infusion of traditions—seders, Purim costumes, synagogue visits, reading the Tanach.

Learning languages—English, French, Hebrew, Yiddish. Being a polyglot. Blossoming, becoming. Drawing, swimming, living in a belated childhood, becoming my own person. Glorious can mean ascent, elevation, dignity. All entered my life here in Montreal. I was renamed, but also reborn as a Jewishly educated child with a known future informed by my own, heretofore lost, heritage. Again leaving, grieving. At least anticipating revisiting them.

Gloria at the last stop, New York. New last name, Bernstein. But real *mishpachah* (family)aunt, uncle, and cousins become Mom, Pop, and brothers. Surgically having my eyes straightened; growing up, becoming American, young adult, college student, teacher. The Holocaust behind me, life ahead of me.

Gloria Glantz: More becoming. Becoming a wife, creating, and a family. *Glantz*, a Yiddish word that means to shine, to glow. Enjoying motherhood, learning something each new day, revisiting the early storms of my life, reaching the souls of children through my teaching. Writing, revising, giving, and reliving. What is in a name? A sliver of your life.

My life is not glorious, but neither is it inglorious. I will not stoop to those low depths of my hangmen but will reach for the unreachable heights. I will not be twisted by hate but will teach acceptance and respect. I will not always be successful but just striving for it is success.

So the life of Gitele informs the life of Mother Goose. I am Gitl, Chanusha, Gucia, Guta, Gloria, and Mother Goose. I am good, glorious, full, rhymed, and playful. Though nearly gone yesterday, I am here today. I will be here tomorrow through those I affect today. Therefore, I am a *Yad Vashem*, a witness, an everlasting name. I am a voice in the emerging light, only a whisper of those who cannot speak.

Gitl Przepiorka, Gloria Bernstein, Gloria Glantz, Mother Goose—I have floated across the continents, have learned to laugh and sing. I strive for perfection because I was given the gift of life multiple times. I was once Gitele.

May I Please Tell You 'bout Miracles

May I tell you who I am and who I'm not,
What I have, and what I haven't got,
What I want, what I don't want,
And what I wonder about
The wormy waste of war has not made me nameless,
I am not, nor will I ever be, nameless
Nor am I only about the darkness of the Shoah,
I am more than this.
I am a living testament to what is possible,
When others see the worth of each,
And bring a light into the death-filled darkness,
If you plow my inner landscape,
There is the mulch of miracles to be found
Of random meetings, loving beginnings, mournful leavings
Lovely and enduring life, and love stories.
Of places and times that should not have coalesced,
Of serendipity, being with who it was, wherever it was.
Of staying alive thirteen miles from Charna Droga,
The black road of Treblinka,
To thriving within five miles of the Long Island's own Rodeo Drive,
Of going from childhood games of hide and seek
To seeking to live by hiding.
Of families that were not mine, but were more mine than not,
Of crowns from flowers that grew on dirt roads
To flowers in lavish bouquets and gorgeous centerpieces.

Of asking "Am I a big girl yet?"
To surviving to becoming one, more miracle than meant to be.
Of giving voice to those abruptly stilled
And being a voice of those whose poems were never written.
If you plow my inner landscape
You will find *The Birdsong*, a poem by a child in Therezin,
Who never emerged from there.
But I, just as he did,
Believe that "the world is filled with loveliness."
And also "know how good it is to be alive."
To honestly believe that
After the nameless graves of Auschwitz and Treblinka,
Is, in itself, a miracle.

Looking Back, Why Did I Survive?

Why did I survive? I don't know why. I should have been the first to die. The youngest were the most useless. I couldn't do any work. I couldn't contribute to the coffers of the Germans. I was an extra mouth to feed. If I had gone to Treblinka with my mother, I would have gone right into the gas chambers together, immediately upon arrival. My brother Zelig, thirteen, begged the neighbors to take him in and hide him. He went by himself and made the desperate requests. "You're a Zhid (Jewish male)." "You look like a Zhid." "Why should I risk my life for a Zhid!" Those were the answers. I was a Zhidovka (Jewish female). I looked like a Zhidovka. They took me in. I didn't have to ask. Being the child of Esther and Mendl Przepiorka was enough. My father had the little leather factory in town and was highly respected. Many of the Polish teenagers got their apprenticeships there. But Zelig, too, was the son of Esther and

Mendl Przepiorka. He was the bright and handsome son. I was cross-eyed and showed no extraordinary promise. I lived. He died.

So many were betrayed, so many shot by cooperative, Nazi-sympathizing Poles. My aunt Esther Breindl was caught by the Gestapo as she tried to get food for her family in hiding. She was tortured for a week before she died without divulging her family's hiding place. So much for going like lambs to the slaughter. My Uncle Joseph survived in the woods until the end of the war and then was shot by Polish police. Someone must have told the German soldiers where to look so they could appear in the middle of the night with flashlights to catch a Jew in hiding. Did they really believe that I, with my dark, crossed eyes and black curly hair was the illegitimate child of a blonde, blue-eyed, and beautiful young Polish woman? And what Catholic woman in staunchly Catholic Poland in the early 1940s would even admit to having an illegitimate grandchild? Logic played a very small role.

And after the war, having survived, what should my life have been? I should have been baptized, continued living with Pania Kowalczyk and going to the big church in the town square. Perhaps I would have finished elementary school, married young, and contributed a Ztajek and a Maria to the Polish Communist proletariat.

There were more miracles. How was I discovered across the continents? The serendipitous meeting by my Aunt Norma of an American soldier from New York! What were the chances that Phil Kaplan, who was part of the American Army's administration of Foehrenwald D.P. Camp, would be in the same room at the moment my Aunt decided to yell out "Esther! Max! Bernstein! Bronx! New York!" over and over again? That this tall, pleasant-looking soldier would speak to her in his broken Yiddish and tell her that the Bernsteins were his neighbors in the Bronx?

If that wasn't enough, there were more unlikely events in my childhood. Living in four countries, having four mothers and two institutions—orphanages—as mother, becoming a miniature polyglot, at one point around age nine, speaking or at least understanding six languages! And blessed with so much love from family and even from strangers!

I survived but lost the experiences of childhood; I survived and recouped my childhood. My eyes were swollen, my cheeks tear-stained, and I was quiet and shy; now I laugh a lot, am interested and outgoing. I am Gitl, Gucia, Guta, Gloria. Mother Goose. I am, quite simply, a lucky woman. I am not a guilty one, for I never caused anyone else's death by living. I do not have survivor guilt. I only have regrets.

Why did I survive? Some questions have no answers. But my survivor status carries with it its own special effects. I work at everything very diligently and try to be the best Gloria I can be, so I'll be worthy of having outlived everyone else in my family, probably by age four. I don't like to relocate; I've moved around enough already. I lived so I must do something useful with my life and do it well.

Did I survive to teach about the useless, tragic deaths? Was it to perpetuate my Judaism? Was it to remember the righteous? Was it to fulfill the commandment to "be fruitful and multiply," to have children, children who have no grandparents, aunts, uncles, or cousins on my side of the family? Was it to defy the edict that marked me for death? Was it my victory and the victory of the Jewish people to teach tolerance and love and show what hate can do but not get down to the level of the killers and preach vengeance and hate?

Truly, there is no rhyme or reason. Randomness and good fortune, just part of an imperfect world and, to my uncomprehending eyes, God's illogical plan.

CHAPTER 6

SURVIVING ONCE MORE

I was due for a mammogram in April of 1993. I actually did not go for one at that time. I found out that I was the recipient of a fellowship from the American Gathering of Jewish Holocaust Survivors, The American Federation of Teachers, and The Jewish Labor Committee to study the Holocaust and Resistance. This enabled me to go to Poland and Israel and study with the most eminent scholars in the field such as Yehuda Bauer, Martin Gilbert, and Michael Berenbaum, among others.

I am remembering again, Wegrow, Poland, July, 1993. The bus stops at a cemetery memorial. The Holocaust and Jewish Resistance Teachers Program trip with approximately forty-five teachers are on a fellowship program to Poland and Israel for in depth study. Benjamin Meed, who organized the trip with his wife Vladka says, "Everyone will stay on the bus, only Gloria will get off. We don't want to antagonize the natives."

View: The visible trace of the existence of centuries-
old Jewish communities in Wegrow.

There is a monument on Berka Joselewicza Street honoring citizens of the town who were murdered by the Nazis during World War
II. It is built with tombstones from the old cemetery. Its central part
consists of the Ten Commandments tablets with the inscription in
Polish and Hebrew, "DO NOT KILL."

The Hebrew text reads: "To the eternal memory of the Jewish community of Wengrow that was annihilated at the hands of the Nazis in the years of the Holocaust 1939-1944." (http://kehilalinks.jewishgen.org/Wegrow/cem-ven.html #17)

There are stones in the unkempt, unruly, weedy grass. A memorial, inscribed in Polish: "You shall not kill." There are broken head stones with parts of names. All around are wild, yellow, purple, pink, and white flowers. They have not been planted here. They just grow freely.

I pick one up and hold it in my hand. I am no longer an adult on a study seminar. I am now in this town, Wegrow, and I am someone else. It is no longer 1993, but 1944. I am catapulted back to the scene of making flower crowns with *Matka*.

The flowers are from the side of the unpaved roadway. They sway, they grow; they were picked by a curiously silent child who just wanted something pretty, something to fill the uneventful, lonely days without other children to play with. Her *Matka* was her only playmate.

In another continent, some fifty years later, during a Passover Seder and as a tribute to the Foundation for the Righteous, I included this tribute to *Matka*:

The flowers will die in a day, or two, or three. The child will live 'til no longer a child. *Matka* will not know her after her childhood.

Matka will no longer get flower crowns, nor will she have anyone to create them with. She will have only her memories.

But later, on her grave, she will have the wild flowers. Who tends your gravesite, dear *Matka*? Your daughter and your husband predeceased you. Your Gucia has left so long ago to another continent.

But the flowers will be there. Year after year they will tell your truth. You did not fear; you bravely persevered. You did not shirk from the human touch, you saved a life, two, three lives. "It is as though you saved the world entire."

The flowers will attest to it. They crown your grave with natural beauty, as was your beauty from within. There will be their swaying heads, their luscious colors, just as you valued luscious life. The potent primary purples, the paler pinks, the sunlit yellows, the bright whites.

All the wild ones growing freely. They will form the crown on your final resting place. The crowns of your caring and consummate courage, the fitting, free flowers of your unforgettable feats.

In my excitement and planning for that compelling trip, I let the appointment lapse *until* I returned from that trip. Or was I so anxious to go on that trip that I feared the mammo? What if something was found and I couldn't accept this opportunity?

I was sitting in my kitchen reading the newspaper and had rested my right hand on the top of my chest when I thought I felt a small lump on the top of my right breast. I touched it more carefully. A lump. I made an appointment for a mammography the following week. The first words the doctor said were: "Are you here by yourself?" After I nodded, he asked, "Do you want to call someone?" I chose not to call Miles because I felt this news should not be delivered on the phone, but when we were together and could hug one another. My emotion then could be most accurately as stunned or frozen. I did not cry. It was November, about two weeks before Thanksgiving and we had a Bar Mitzvah in Montreal that weekend.

Surgery was scheduled for a mastectomy; there were also two positive nodes found. I had reconstruction done on my right breast at the same time.

Craig was taking the LSAT exams for law school, so all I told him was that we'd be in Montreal for a Bar Mitzvah, so there was no need to call. In truth, I didn't want him to hear a hospital announcement, paging a doctor. Like most mothers, I was trying to protect him. He didn't need this news at such an important time for him. When he finally came home after the requisite questions—How was it? Did you find it hard?—I related the results of the mammography. He didn't show any anger that I hadn't told him earlier, only concern. "Oh Mom! Will you be all right?" Then he observed, "This place looks like a funeral parlor." There were so many floral bouquets in the house.

Jordana had been in England at London Guild Hall University on her spring semester abroad from August through December 1993. I had cancer surgery November 1993 but didn't tell her while she was abroad. When she returned, she saw all the flowers in the house. I told her the truth. She cried audibly, visibly devastated. But she was also angry that she wasn't told earlier. In addition, she explained recently, this was a very tough semester for her. Miles' mother, her Grandma Rose, had died while she was in London and she couldn't be at the funeral. She did mail her written tribute to her grandma and requested that Craig read it at the funeral. The rabbi said his own words were no longer necessary, she had said all that should be said about her grandmother.

I started chemo in early January 1994. Within three weeks, I lost all my hair. This was a gut-wrenching experience which brought me back to an earlier traumatic time in my life:

People always told me I had beautiful hair. "Is your hair naturally curly?" "You're so lucky." "It's so thick. It's like fur." Sometimes women would follow me. "Where do you have your hair cut?" I have always worn it the same length, fairly short. I can comb it with my hands. It is literally carefree.

This view of my hair is ingrained into my psyche, though I didn't really know how much. I know I took it for granted and always wanted what I couldn't have—straight hair. At one point "falls" (a hairpiece of long, straight hair which you put over your own hair) were popular, and I got one which totally changed my appearance. In addition, I even took a long trek from the Bronx to a beauty shop in Brooklyn to have my kinks and curls straightened. I hated the result and couldn't wait for the reappearance of those kinks and curls.

Now I realize I didn't value or fully appreciate my dark thick mop until life gave me a jolt, suddenly making me exquisitely aware of my mortality.

After the second chemotherapy treatment in late January of 1994, I was told my hair would begin falling out. It already looked lifeless, and there were many stray hairs on my sweaters and jackets. I was prepared, I thought. I had a one-thousand-dollar wig and a cheaper one as well. I had snoods and caps. I already considered myself a survivor. I would survive this, too. An avid walker and swimmer, I had foregone the visit to the JCC to swim with Miles this one particular night and decided to stay home. I was warm and comfortable on my taupe velvet couch. The étagères were filled with family pictures and books and artwork I loved was on the walls.

I put my hand through my hair as I often had done. There in my hand was my beautiful, naturally curly, thick hair! Then another handful and another! I felt my scalp. It was bare! And then it happened—the agonizing, heaving, breathless keening, and the tightness in my chest as if a clamp had suddenly stopped my heart from beating! The loud wail escaped from my lips. My whole body was shaking wildly, desperately, and uncontrollably. I recognized it! I was no longer in my commodious home. It was fifty years earlier! I was in Wegrow, Poland, in a small and unfamiliar farmhouse, a house which was not my home, with a man on a cross on the wall and a picture of a beautifully draped woman on a painting, a wooden tub in the kitchen, my small, blue cardboard suitcase on the floor. I was three years old at Maria Kowalczyk's, a woman I did not know. I was now feeling the same helplessness and utter despair I had experienced as that night in 1942, when a woman with a beautiful voice, my dark-eyed, ashen-faced mother, left me. Forever.

Not ever before that January 1994 evening or since have I experienced that body clenching, gut-wrenching feeling. It was so recognizable. The gut never forgets.

I had a beautiful "real hair" wig for daytime, but I was wearing a snood at night to keep my head warm as I slept.

One night about ten o'clock when I was already in bed, the doorbell rang. Miles answered it. Who was it? Jordana walked into the bedroom! I was shocked! Of course, I was thrilled to see her but I didn't want to scare her with my appearance. Miles knew she was coming and was sworn to secrecy. She had asked a friend to pick her up at the airport so Miles wouldn't have to. She was so kind about the way I looked. "You look nice, Mom. How are you feeling?" A complete surprise, a beautiful gesture. I was going to survive this, too.

Suddenly, the everyday concerns became less important. For example, about two months before this, I had ordered a new car. A red Honda! As I was sitting in the living room reading one afternoon, the doorbell rang. I answered it and was told my new Honda was being delivered. I looked out. I didn't see a red car, I saw a black one! "Is this my car?" I asked. "It's the wrong color; I ordered red!" Here I was, bald as a bowling ball, just diagnosed and operated on for breast cancer, now on chemotherapy. I wasn't going to make an issue of *this!* So I got the black Honda. I drove it for twelve years!

When I completed the treatments, I had a celebratory party for my colleagues at school and other friends who had been so kind to me. While I still hate going for mammograms, I have been cancer free for twenty-four years!

CHAPTER 7

LIFTING THE BURDEN FROM MY HEART

Miles and I took an Eastern European vacation with Tauck Tours beginning on August 14, 2004. We Visited Warsaw, Krakow, Budapest, Vienna, and Prague. Of course, we enjoyed the old churches and synagogues, the Chain Bridge in Budapest, the Klezmer bands in Krakow, the Monument to the Heroes of the Warsaw ghetto uprising in Warsaw. Poland, the country of my birth, evoked some memories that had not surfaced for more than sixty years. We went to Old Town in Warsaw. Warsaw was reduced to rubble by German bombing and was reconstructed in 1945, according to 17th and 18th century style. Outlines and paintings were available as an aid to the reconstruction.

http://www.warszawaguide.info/Gamle%20byEng/index.html citation #7

I remember walking through that rubble! Why was I in Warsaw at age seven? I was leaving the orphanage in Otwock, Poland. Again music was evocative: *Warszawa ty moja kochana*, or, loosely translated, *Warsaw, You are My Sweetheart*. Were the Poles singing this song after the destruction of Warsaw in the hope it would be their thriving city again? The first few bars of that song reverberate in my throat still.

http://www.warszawaguide.info/Gamle%20
byEng/index.htm Citation #8

Being in Poland, hearing Polish, my mother tongue, spoken and recalling the rubble, I found myself thinking about my childhood in Wegrow, and my family, especially my grandmother Rachel and grandfather Pinchas. I imagined being able to visit my grandparents' home again after an eternity. The following is my imaginary visit and a figment of my imagination since I would not remember their home. A Yiddish song I love, *Vu is dos Gesele* was the genesis of this piece.

Vu is dos Gesele, vu is die shtieb. Where is the little street? Where is the house? The words of a song fit very well. I am standing on the little street in front of the house. This is the little street, this is the small house. I went to the chamber of commerce, got the address, a young woman interpreter, and we walked there. Sixty-five years ago, my grandmother and grandfather had lived here.

I peeked in the door, slightly ajar. First, I saw the light bulb in the ceiling. Then the wooden bench in the corner. Then I noticed the floor, bare and scratched. The green rug was no longer there. Grandma Rachel would sweep up the crumbs and then use a brush to clean it. She'd put it outside and bang it with a wooden frond. She would shampoo it weekly. There couldn't be a hair, a pebble, or a stain on it. It had to be spotless, especially for Shabbat. We, children, always were admonished to take our shoes off to walk on it. According to Aunt Norma, my grandmother's fetish was cleanliness. She had passed it on to two of her daughters Norma and Esther.

We knocked on the door. We told her we were walking in the neighborhood and this house has a special meaning for us because my grandparents had lived here. Could we come in and refresh our special memories? The toothless woman beckoned us to come in.

A red, drooping geranium plant now occupied the corner shelf. Once, my grandmother's gorgeous yellow plate stood there on a plate stand. It came off the shelf only for gefilte fish, with a circle of bright green parsley surrounding the fish. The plate looked bordered in green, thought it was all yellow, with different textures of glaze designed on it. Whenever we walked into the room and saw the plate missing from the corner shelf, we knew there was gefilte fish for dinner.

In this house had been the yeasty smell of *challah*, the full-bodied aroma of fresh chicken soup, and the sweet, cinnamon scent of *lokshn kugel* (noodle pudding). Now dampness and strong coffee permeated the air.

We didn't have a long conversation. "How long are you here?" "A long time. It was my brother's house. He willed it to me. He moved here in 1942. It was a good buy then. I've been here all this time. No, I didn't know the previous owner."

My charm bracelet jingled. I looked down on it. My favorite gold charm in the form of little pages in a book has the priestly benediction, *Yiverecheha Adonai v' 'ishmerehah, Yaer Adonai*. It is on my grandmother's bracelet. These were also the words of grandpa who blessed us each Friday night before we went home, "May you be like Menasheh and Ephraim, Sarah Leah, Rachel and Rebecca (fore-mothers names added in the Reform tradition)." That's a tall order.

We did not stay long. I took a wistful look at the peeling wall. Even the white marble fireplace is not elegant any more. Warmth it does not exude. A long brown crack cascades down the upper mantle ledge.

Yes, *ot is dos gesele.* (Here is the little street), *Ot is die shtieb,* (here is the house).

And yet it isn't. And will never again be for me.

I was also thinking of *Matka* again after almost sixty years. I felt the heavy heart of unfinished business: thanking *Matka* for saving me. I remembered all her good deeds that allowed me to survive Hitler's hell. I was moved to compose a tribute to her.

Ode to Matka

When Mendl's pleas and Esther's walk took Gitl
to your care,
You were there.
When tested by tyrants during her prayer, was
her life worthy of life?
You were there.
When dancing could save me, or cut my
tomorrows,
You were there.
When we slept with the earthworms, and ate
hard potatoes,
You were there.
When I had to learn my ABC, with too many
letters there for me,
You were there.

With kielbasa and bread, songs of birds flying
free, with uncommon bravery,
You were there
But where are you now?
We're so far apart,
I can't feel your grace,
As I don't see your face.
But truly, I see it still,
Till the end of my days, I know I will.
You are there, in my heart. Always there.

However, even after this memory, I felt the heavy heart of unfinished business. I had to thank her for saving me.

That opportunity arose a few years later. In 2010, I received a letter from the Hidden Child Foundation that Dr. Mordecai Paldiel, who had headed the Righteous Among the Nations Department at Yad Vashem for twenty-four years, was now retired from that position and was teaching at Stern College in New York City. That letter further indicated he would be willing to help any survivor honor his or her rescuer. Within a day, I wrote to him, outlining the events of my early life. The next day we made an appointment to meet. There were more meetings, like seeing the Friedmans at their home in New Jersey, with me in New York City, e-mail communications, Yad Vashem questions and responses. Eventually it became a reality. In a letter dated April 29, 2013, we were notified that Marianna and Michal Kowalczyk were awarded the title "Righteous Among the Nations" (Show letter in appendix).

Marianna Podgorska Kowalczyk (1897- 12/29/87 (died at 90) (p. 47 of Part V)
Place during the war: Wegrow, Wegrow, Lublin, Poland
Rescue Place: Wegrow, Wegrow, Lublin, Poland

Rescue mode: Hiding

File number: File from the Collection of the Righteous Among the Nations

Department (M.31.2/12517)

Commemoration

Date of Recognition: 17/02/2013

Rescued Persons

Glantz, Przepiorka, Gloria, Gitl; Starr, Frydman, Maryla; Frydman, Semiontek, Malka http://db.yadvashem.org/righteous/family. html?language=en&itemid=9797716 (source # for rescue story below)

Kowalczyk FAMILY Kowalczyk Marianna (1897-1986)

Kowalczyk Michal, husband

Rescue Story

Gitl Przepiorka was born in Wegrow in 1939 to Mendl and Ester Przepiorka who had two older sons. The parents and the older siblings all died in Trebiinka. Before being taken there in 1942, Ester took little Gitl to the home of Marianna and Michal Kowalczyk, whom she had known before the war and who had agreed to take the little girl.

At the time of their separation, Gitl cried and clung to her mother, but Marianna was warm and gentle with her. Eventually, the child adjusted to her new home and started calling Marianna "*Matka*" (mother).

Who was this person, Marianna (or Maria) Kowalczyk?

She was an ordinary, religious, church-going Catholic woman living in the countryside of Wegrow. Though her education probably did not exceed third grade, her intelligence was evidenced in her resourcefulness, intuition, and her cleverness in being able to lie and make logical arguments so her fabricated stories would not reveal dangerous truths. In addition, though always in danger, she was caring and courageous. Her husband, Michau (on Hebrew document, Michal), was the caretaker on the property of the leather factory owned by my father. They always got along well and had no disagreements. As a matter of fact, my father had even lent him money, which he repaid.

We lived in the same courtyard, and the Kowalczyks had known me from the day I was born. Since my Hebrew name was Chane Gitl, I was called Gitl, or affectionately Gitele, which translated into Gucia in Polish. The Chaneh she changed to Chanusha, and that's what she called me before the Germans entered Wegrow.

It is most illuminating to hear from Marianna herself, the description of her life after the Nazis entered Wegrow. Through the good graces of the Jewish Historical Institute in Warsaw I was able to get a description of her life and mine, as well as our feelings during that period.

Marianna hid three Jews; Maryla, whom she called Stefcia; Friedman, (now Marilyn Starr); and her mother Malka Friedman, as well as me, Gitl Przepiorka. She called me Gucia to hide my Jewish identity, and my name now became a Christian name, Gucia Kowalczyk. I was supposed to be her daughter's child from an illicit relationship, I called her *Matka* just like her daughter called her *Matka*.

Although my father had asked Michal to take me in, he was already dead when his request was granted, so he would never know that his precious princess would live.

Even though she had known my family and me from birth, she fabricated a story about how I suddenly appeared in her yard one night—an adorable two- or three-year-old little girl who spoke such good Polish! In addition, fully aware how many of her countrymen harbored very negative and anti-Semitic feelings toward Jews, she made certain that her beautiful and flirtatious daughter Stanka would actually report this incident to a virulent anti-Semite, Hanczyn, so he wouldn't hear about it elsewhere and then start doing his own research, and perhaps uncover the truth. She exhibited this craftiness and mendacity for a good purpose. She even kept the truth from members of her own family who she felt would not take kindly to her generosity toward Jews such as her anti-Semitic sister-in-law who lived in the village, and her mother-in-law who lived in the same house with her. Her mother-in-law actually went into the attic and discovered the Friedmans. So how did Maria prevent this old lady from going into the countryside and talking about it to her Jew-hating daughter?

She came up with an ingenious plan to keep her mother-in law at home. They had chicken, and everyone knows that the eggs had to be kept warm. Just as chickens sit on their eggs to keep them warm so that chicks can hatch easily, she made her mother-in-law stay in bed all day to warm the eggs-like a good mother hen!

Yes, truth can sometimes be stranger than fiction.

And even her husband, Michau, did not know that Maryla Friedman was moved into the attic after seven months in the barn! She kept the Friedmans in the barn and the attic for a total of one and a half years, from 1942 to almost September 1944. She washed their clothes and fed them first. She also protected Arnold, and Morris, Maryla's two brothers who had false papers. Arnold came around sporadically, so she told her neighbors that he (Joseph was his false name) was her daughter's fiancé.

Yet there was another less obvious reason for keeping her family unsuspecting. Knowing the punishments for people helping Jews, she thought to herself, *If they will not know, and only I will know, then they will kill only me, and not my husband or my daughter.* Of course, people who were hiding Jews were sometimes more afraid of their neighbors than of the Nazis. If the neighbors knew of a hidden Jew and didn't report it, they were implicated and guilty just like the rescuer! It boggles my mind to see that if one betrayed someone he was rewarded, usually with the Jew's clothing, but if he didn't betray and acted humanely, he would be shot.

We might have asked her, "Marianna, these were people you knew and liked, so you do not regret having helped them. But Marianna, you saved others who were strangers. You went into the ghetto in the middle of the night to warn them that the next day the ghetto would be liquidated! Complete strangers! You can answer truthfully. Why did you risk your life for complete strangers?" And she would say, "I risked my life saving three people I had known, I lived in a state of severe fright daily, but I couldn't turn them away. I didn't do it for payment, but I couldn't turn them away. And I do not regret it to this day."

Marianna Kowalczyk, my dear *Matka*, I wish I could have nominated you for sainthood. Maria's description of her love for me and my devotion to her are equally moving.

Butchinsky had a restaurant in a suburban part of Wegrow and that is where he kept my cousin Fishl, hiding him in the ice cellar, and that is where Aunt Norma went after she jumped off the train on the way to Treblinka. Butchinsky was also one of the righteous people who had to live in fear and hide and probably lie to his neighbors.

https://en.pons.com/translate/polish-english/strach+ma+wielkie+oczy *Strach ma wiellkieoczy.* Fear makes things look twice as bad as they are.

Our feelings for each other are best illustrated by our reactions to our separation from each other.

Maria had promised my mother that if she and my father died, she would send me to my aunt in America. She got my aunt's address and, as proof of my survival, had me write my Aunt Esther a letter and enclose a picture of myself (in the pretty outfit). Aunt Esther engaged an agent from the Polish Jewish Committee to get me to America and my *Matka* brought me to Janowice and then to Wroclaw, where Jewish children were boarding the plane. She writes that she will never forget that parting. "My Hanusia, when she was the only one entering the plane, suddenly, in shock, bolted out of the plane crying and screaming, 'Save me mother! Where are they taking me?'" Can anyone imagine her feelings then? She who had cherished and loved me with her whole heart, raised me as her own child, who had endangered her life for me and because of me, was letting me go, keeping her promise to my murdered parents. She was very tortured about her decision to give me up. She loved me very much, but she knew my Aunt Esther and Uncle Max were rich and could give me all that I deserved because I was talented and bright. On the other hand, the Friedmans told her that I would surely be kidnapped anyway because Jews who survived knew they would probably not be recognized by their children, so they would kidnap them from Christian rescuers. So she might as well give me to my wealthy auntie. Do I owe this woman any debt of gratitude? I address this question fully in another chapter. She lived to the age of ninety, so I had many years to be of help to her. Unfortunately, that has not been my path and for seventy years, that regret has burdened me and weighed heavily on my heart. I should have had tantrums and ignored my new families and written to her.

But I was a child who did exactly as I was told. I had to follow all the rules. If I didn't, I could have been killed, and killed *Matka's* family.

When I already had my own family, I was put in touch with the Friedman family through my cousin Fishl when he visited us from Israel in 1977. We visited them in New Jersey, and I felt this was an opportunity to communicate with my rescuer. So I took pictures of my family and asked the Friedmans, who, unlike me, were still fluent in Polish, to write to her. They agreed to do so. They even mentioned to me that they had told her I had gone to college that I was married and had two children and leading a good life. I was sure that this knowledge would have made her proud. And I surmised that a few words from me accompanied by photos would be a boon to her lonely existence.

The years passed. I felt good that I had finally written to her and was not upset when I didn't get an answer because I knew she was already in her later years and possibly couldn't write any more. When I took my kids, college students by then, to the Hidden Child Gathering in New York in 1991, I looked forward to getting an update from the Friedmans, or even from *Matka* about how she felt when she got my dictated letter and pictures. Imagine my sorrow and anger when they related that they hadn't written the note after all! I was devastated and angry at the same time! They had taken it upon themselves to judge that she might have been more upset getting this late mail from me after my not having written to her for so many years. They made that decision for me and I felt the black rage rising within me. But no! The anger should have been directed at myself! I now had her address! I could have asked someone with good Polish skills to write to her! *I* was at fault! And, unfortunately, she had already died when this meeting took place.

My dear *Matka,* I can no longer give you the thanks that you deserve. Please forgive me, *moja kochana Matka.*

Citations on the translations pieces 0011 and 0010

About 515 people of all races, ages, and ethnicities have gathered to attend an event titled A Light in the Darkness in the sanctuary of the Community Synagogue in Port Washington, on Sunday, November 24, 2013. Among the guests were, of course, members of the immediate and extended families of the Glantz's and the Friedmans. But also Hunter High School Alumni Linda, Barbara, and Sunny; teaching colleagues from the Manhasset School District from as far away as Vermont, including Connie and Peter Frank; volunteers; docents; and leaders of the HMTC, including chairman Steven Markowitz; Senior Director of Education, Beth Lilach; and my editor, Emily Berkowitz; clergy of the Community Synagogue, Rabbi Irwin Zeplowitz; Cantor Claire Franco; President Jack Mandell and many other congregants; members of the senior group, *Chaverim* with chairpersons, Evie and Les Schonbrun, and others who contributed their encouragement and time and effort in baking and providing refreshments. Attending were also many guests of all religions and persuasions, providing a rich rainbow of diverse colors and hues to our gathering. I want to add that it was Rabbi Zeplowitz's idea to have this event at the Community Synagogue. When I told him my rescuer was honored by Yad Vashem, he was very excited and offered, "Let's have it here." And it was fortuitous that we did, since the Holocaust Center could not have accommodated a crowd of 515 people—the largest crowd at the Community Synagogue ever assembled there—with the exception of Yom Kippur services!

The event was publicized as a "unique, interfaith community event." It was exactly that and more. It was a testament to a woman who dared to challenge the hate around her and respond with love, caring and daring, even though it meant putting herself and her family in danger.

A Light in the Darkness

The Community Synagogue
160 Middle Neck Road, Port Washington, NY
Sunday, November 24, 2013, 1:30 PM
Co-sponsors:
Holocaust Memorial and Tolerance Center
The Community Synagogue of Port Washington
Polish American Museum
AJC - Global Jewish Advocacy
JCRC - Jewish Community Relations Council

The speakers at the event were Dr. Mordecai Paldiel; Gloria Glantz, the survivor who was cared for by Maria Kowalczyk; and Eva Junczyk- Ziomecka, the consul general of Poland.

THE SPEAKERS

Dr. Mordecai Paldiel headed the Righteous Among the Nations Department at Yad Vashem from 1982–2007 and was himself rescued from the Holocaust by a righteous gentile. He earned his MA and PhD at Temple University in the field of Religious and Holocaust studies. His books include *The Path of the Righteous, Sheltering the Jews, Saving the Jews, Diplomat Heroes of the Holocaust*, and *The Righteous Among the Nations*. He currently teaches at Stern College and Drew University and serves as a consultant to the International Raoul Wallenberg Foundation.

Gloria Glantz, born in Wegrow, Poland, was rescued by the Kowalczyks, being honored today. She got her BA at Hunter College, MA at Columbia University, and MBA at Adephi University. She has developed and taught Holocaust and tolerance workshops for teachers in many Long Island school districts and has won the Anne Frank Outstanding Educator Award, and The Holocaust and Resistance Fellowship to study in Israel and Poland. Gloria frequently speaks to children and adults at various educational and religious institutions.

Ewa Junczyk-Ziomecke is the consul general of the Republic of Poland in New York. She has served as secretary of state at the Chancellery of the President of the Republic of Poland in charge of social issues. In August 1980, she was at the Gdansk Shipyard during the solidarity-ignited strike. During the martial law in Poland, she was officially banned by the communist regime from working as a journalist. In 1982, Junczyk-Ziomecka joined the émigré community of the former Solidarity members in the USA.

In 2005, she became the deputy director of the Museum of the History of Polish Jews and was responsible for contracts with the Jewish and Polish communities in the United States, and the promotion of the Museum in Poland and abroad.

Through the good auspices of Dr. Paldiel, I was able to have a copy of Marianna and Michal Kowalczyk's honoring certificate sent to me from Yad Vashem. After Dr. Paldiel presented it to me, I, with tears in my eyes, presented it to our children Craig and Jordana.

Dear Craig, Dear Jordana,

I feel so fortunate to present to you this honoring certificate. It was earned because of the heroism of a most deserving couple, Marianna and Michal Kowalczyk, now named Righteous Among the Nations. You are not only the keepers of their legacy. You are their legacy. They made you possible. I am confident you will live up to the qualities that made them our heroes; being on the side of justice, caring, understanding, tolerance and acceptance. I hope it will always be a reminder to you, of the power of love, humanity and goodness. I know you will pass on these qualities to your children as you already are doing.

With love,
Mom

We hugged. I felt their warm tears on my cheek.

Certificate of Honor (translation below)
This certificate establishes that from the
7th day of Adar 5773 (February 17, 2013)
The Commission for the Designation of the
"Righteous Among the Nations"
Through the authority of the Memorial of *Yad Vashem*
By the witnesses that appeared before us,
decided to honor and recognize
Marianna and Michal Kowalczyk
Who, during the years of the Holocaust in Europe
put their lives at risk to save Jews who
were fleeing from their pursuers,
and
To grant them the medal of
"The Righteous Among the Nations"
Their names will forever be extolled on the Wall
of Honor in the Garden of the "Righteous
Among the Nations"
At *Yad Vashem*.
Hereby attested to in Jerusalem
20th of Iyar 5773 (April 30, 2013)
Avner Shalev
Through the authority of the Memorial of Yad Vashem
Jacob Turkel
On behalf of the Commission for the Designation of the Righteous

On the same afternoon at that event, I summarized what hate had done.

What if: Germans had listened to the bad conscience of the White Rose movement, brave German teens and their professors, and turned against Hitler instead of betraying those kids and allowing them to be hanged for their courage-

What if: The thirty-two nations at the Evian Conference called by President Franklin Roosevelt in July 1938 had said, "Yes, we'll take the émigrés from Germany, Austria?"

What if: the Wagner Rogers bill had not died in committee and 20,000 Jewish children were allowed to enter the USA in February 1939?What if: The 932 passengers on the St. Louis, rejected by Cuba, were allowed to land in Miami?

What if: Neighbor had not turned against neighbor.

What if, what if, what if? Then we would not have had the following statistics. As a result of hate, indifference, intolerance, insensitivity, and inhumanity:

- Approximately 6,000,000 Jews were killed. One and a half million of which were children;
- According to the USHMM, thousands of Polish civilians and 1,748 Polish priests were Jewish killed in executions or in forced labor, and concentration camps;
- About 4,500 Polish children were kidnapped to Germany for reeducation. Some stats report up to 100,000 Polish "Aryan" children were kidnapped under the Lebensbom program. (an SS program devised to propagate Aryan traits) http://www.nytimes.com/2006/11/07/world/europe/07nazi.html Citation # 9 (Your father, your son, your sister, your brother, your grandfather, your best friend.)
- Between 200,000–500,000 Roma & Sinti (4,000 in Auschwitz alone) died.
- People with disabilities, those unworthy of life, were brutally targeted. Between 200,000 and 275,000 people with

mental and physical disabilities were murdered between 1939–1945. Between 300,000 and 400,000 were sterilized in that time period.

- Five thousand to 15,000 homosexuals were killed. Fifteen thousand gay men were imprisoned, thousands killed (per Yad Vashem); however, countless gays and lesbians were murdered because so few gay people at that time identified themselves as gay. Nazi records only cover the gays they identified. (Your mother, your daughter, your grandmother, your best friend.)
- Four hundred to five hundred black children were sterilized, and some murdered outright or died due to unsanitary sterilization procedures. (Those fathered by French Colonial troops, black soldiers with German women during WWI.) (Your parent, your child, your sister, your brother, your grandparent, your best friend.)

That is what indifference, intolerance, insensitivity, and inhumanity did.

Calling up all the descendants of the Friedman and Glantz families to the *bimah* (the platform which houses the Torah) Craig and Jordana presented the most powerful evidence of what the Kowalczyks' courage and love had accomplished. The *bimah*, filled with about twenty-five beaming individuals, would have been bare had it not been for Maria and Michal Kowalczyk.

Craig

Many times over the years, my sister Jordana and I have shared the story of Marianna and Michal Kowalczyk in conversation, through the written word and, most powerfully, through the sharing of our mom's testimony.

It begins, almost unimaginably, with my grandmother Esther Przepiorka walking through the dark woods in the middle of the night to deliver her daughter to two people who were basically strangers in the hope that these two people could somehow ensure her little girl's safety. Without second thought, the Kowalcyzk's opened their home, and their hearts, to that frightened little girl. (And, just as remarkable is how they provided a safe haven to a Jewish teenager and her mother, Maryla, and Malka Friedman).

As we think about this quite unbelievable story, we often wonder whether Marianna and Michal really ever understood the full impact of what they were doing. For example, when Marianna told people that Gitl was her granddaughter to disguise the little girl's true identity, did she ever contemplate that the little girl would someday grow up to raise a family of her own? Did she ever think that the little girl she taught to say prayers to the Virgin Mary would someday influence, as a teacher and educator, thousands of school children?

Did Michal ever imagine that, by providing a loving home to a scared, innocent child, he was passing on a legacy of love and acceptance that would continue way beyond his own years? Did it ever sink in that he was saving a life? Marianna and Michal Kowalczyk were true heroes. We wonder if either of them ever realized that.

The story that you've heard today is often met with disbelief and tears. It is equal parts heartbreak and inspiration wrapped in a lot of luck and immense love. It's the love of two people who, in a time when almost no one would stand up, *did* stand up.

Jordana

As Jordana introduced the members of these two families on the *bimah*, she stated:

Created unknowingly, this is the legacy of Marianna and Michal. Thirteen-year-old Maryla, now Marilyn Starr, still working and running her family pearl business in New York City, her husband Morris, and just some of her children and grandchildren. Marilyn's brother Arnold, fortunate enough to have had false baptismal papers was not hidden and would occasionally visit the Kowalczyk home to see his family—his wife Regina, and just some of their extended family. Then she further went on to introduce our family, children, and grandchildren. A lifetime ahead of them to become who they are meant to be, and yet they would not have been here. There is really no expression of gratitude adequate enough. May we only hope that we can continue to live our lives as they did—with compassion, acceptance, and love for other human beings. Marianna and Michal, we are forever indebted.

Indebted for our lives.

The stone on my heart is less weighty and oppressive. This nest is warmer and more comfortable now.

The End

ENDNOTE

What I won't forgive:

The inhumanity—the gas chambers, starvation, hard useless labor, target practice on our children, our women not good enough to befriend but suitable for rape, the *szmalcownicy*, Polish blackmailers who took your coat or money or reported you to the sentry, the murder of Lidice after the bravery of Czech resistance fighters killed killer Heydrich, those who stood by and let all the cruelty happen.

What I will forgive:

The nameless German soldier who asked for forgiveness, the German soldier who asked for a transfer from killing innocents at the expense of being called a coward. I have no right to forgive anyone else, only those no longer here have that right.

Here is my bitterness:

You took our names, you took our clothes, you took our hair, you took the grandparents and the grandchildren, the beautiful and the plain; you took our books, our holy days and our culture; you took the musicians, the artists, the scientists of yesterday and today; you prevented progress and discovery; you made humans into beasts, back to the darkest ages. You stole my childhood.

Here is my best:

I will not stoop to the level of murderers. I will teach tolerance and acceptance. I will teach about standing up not standing by. I will teach "risk a kind act." I will keep remembrance alive. I will celebrate goodness and worthy heroes. I will express, not hide, my Judaism. I will give Hitler no victory. I will be proud of my gifts to the world—children and grandchildren, my best revenge.

And not really the end:

I hope this incomplete picture of that time, when the world had lost its moral compass, will give some hope to my children and grandchildren that through love and compassion this compass can be restored. Hope and acts of love can move mountains. I hope that within my lifetime, the missing pieces of the puzzles will be found and the mountains will be moved.

ADDENDUM

Remembering and Honoring Loved Ones

Aunt Norma's Funeral Eulogy (2002)

The famous, the rich, the actors, and the politicians have funerals everyone knows about. The unknown, unsung, ordinary; our neighbors, our friends, our own loved ones have funerals that few know about. Only their close friends and family attend. And if they have been blessed with ripe old age, those friends are few.

So it is with Norma Schneiderman, to me, Aunt Norma, not rich or famous, but nevertheless, a heroine. Just a few words about who she was and is for me. A few words of memory and celebration, for she was woman for whom celebration is warranted.

The person who gave me my first doll and carriage was Aunt Norma. She presented it to me in the spring of 1945, having survived the Shoah by having the courage to jump off the train headed for Treblinka. I met her again at the DP camp, her way station to America where she cooked the most wonderful, rich chicken broth I have ever tasted before or since. This was the woman who actually found me. She is the one who connected me with my future in the United States. This is the woman who foiled Hitler's plan not to be alive past her twenty-third birthday. This was her first victory—just surviving.

And what a survival it was. No one knew the meaning of hard work better than Norma. Whether it was making some extra change doing sewing or dressmaking when she got to America or working in her own butcher store with her husband Willie; whether it was keeping her home spotlessly clean (Willie told us she went through two vacuum cleaners her first three years in Florida!); whether it was preparing a scrumptious meal and making sure you had seconds of everything. She'd come with frozen *kreplach* for everyone, and stuffed breast of veal. Our son Craig couldn't get enough of Aunt Norma's *kreplach*! One year when she attended our *seder* (Passover meal), I had to get her fresh fish. Needless to say, that was the best *gefilte* fish we ever had.

Her home always sparkled, for Willie, for her children, her grandchildren, her great-grandchildren, and any visitor who was the recipient of her gracious hospitality. Not only did she survive with strength and dignity, but she left a legacy of great grandchildren as a future generation for our people. She wouldn't allow the Jewish people to become, as Hitler foresaw, an extinct race. This was her second great victory.

For me personally, she was my bond with my past, my connection to a world I came from but never really knew. She was the chain that linked me to my European *shtetl*, Wegrow, the living link to my long-gone parents, siblings, aunts and uncles, and grandparents. She frequently expressed her love for my mother, so in her presence *I* felt loved. And I also felt her affection for my children. Our conversations never ended without "How's Craig? How's Jordana?"

I will always keep your memory for a blessing. May you rest in peace, Aunt Norma.

I spoke and sang at Sam's funeral (He loved the Yiddish song *Vu is Dos Gesele*). He was so good to me and did not believe in organized religion, so we had no rabbi at the funeral. I was the rabbi, assisted by Tova, his stepdaughter.

To the tune of *Vee Is Dos Gesele,* for Sam's funeral
Now that you've left us
It's so hard to part
But your ripe years
Were matched by your big heart,
You were so generous
A fly you'd not hurt,
And off your back
You would give up your shirt!
You were happy with little,
Never asked for more,
Except if good chuck steaks
Were on sale at the store!
Many would marvel,
They never have heard,
An address on e-mail
From an adopted bird!
Heshy was lucky to have you as "dad"
Such gourmet meals no bird
Ever has had!
With you on the dock
And the fat in your hand
That heron Heshy
Was king of the land!
So we say good-bye
Our very dear Sam,
We all love you
Though you were sometimes a ham!
Your moustache a trademark
Your belly too big,
Only because we love you
We'd give you a dig!
Your hearing was dismal

You ate too much meat.
But being with you was,
Always a great treat!

Just as I wrote to the family no longer with me, I want to address the present and future generations, my children and grandchildren.

Happy Father's Day, Craig (2015)—an example of my Hallmark ability according to my husband, Miles.

Perhaps when your son Judah is around thirty, you and Katie will send these words, which we wrote to you, to him.

Never count the years as a burden, they are an invitation and a hope. Just count the blessings and the achievements. You have already felt the sting of tragedy and tasted the sweetness of love. You have the mind to have achieved impressive academic success, and many gifts and talents that can sustain you when you need a mood boost. You have tested yourself in career and life choices and succeeded even when you did not succeed. You constantly learn about yourself, and don't shirk any responsibility to your job, your family, and your friends. You are like a brother to your friends, and a friend to your brothers-in-law and the rest of your family. We could not ever imagine a son as devoted, intelligent, and loving as you are to us.

As the father you are, you are planting the seeds in your children for them to give you the joys a parent gets from his children. Your devotion to Lexi is no less significant. You respect your children, love them, enjoy them, provide for them, and consider them in all your important decisions. No conversation is ever complete without your words: "I love them sooo much!"

True, you will be tested. There will be trying and challenging times. But we know the joys will outweigh those.

Craig, as a father you are the same as you are in all the other roles we play in life. Considerate, loving, hard-working, intelligent, talented, funny, charismatic, resourceful; also driven, tense, sometimes even annoying! (Perfection is only in heaven.)

Enjoy the day and a wonderful year ahead!

With love,
Mom and Dad

Another Hallmark letter below for Jordana's fortieth birthday. Craig, the Prince of Surprises, hand delivered it to her in Atlanta on her fortieth birthday!

April 20, 2013 (date of writing; birthday is April 25, 1973)

Dearest Jordana,

A mother's heart remembers the beautiful face, open eyes looking into her eyes after the initial cry, the well-developed 8-lb. 13-oz. little being that was a mystery and a treasure.

Forty years have passed since then, and we had no way of knowing the heights she would be able to reach.

Within that time, so many accomplishments and blessings! Through the years, the tribulations and the victories, a special woman of intelligence, heart, friendliness, family values, ethics, street smarts, business sense, soft spots and hard spots, but also the right spots would appear!

Jordana, our pride in you only grows as you lead a life of worth passing on to your children good deeds and a concern for the less fortunate; as you know the value of true friendships; as you have created a home filled with activity, and individual fulfillment for each of you. You have made some wonderful choices. You really hit the jackpot when you won Kevin! Our wish for you is that you, Kevin, Maxwell, Emerson, and Kenzie be blessed with good health and prosperity; that you get satisfaction and joy from all that you undertake and have special *naches* (pride and satisfaction) from those beautiful children.

Perfection is never within reach but reaching for it is what counts. May this be a wonderful year for you! Enjoy your birthday and have many more wonderful events for all of us to celebrate.

We love you.

Mom and Dad

Letter to my Oldest Grandson, Maxwell:

Dear Maxwell,

You were our first grandson. That in itself was a special occasion. But there are so many other reasons you are special to us and make us proud.

You are a handsome, strong, and muscular boy, but you are a soft, kind, and gentle person. You always make sure your sisters are safe and Papa is in no danger when he walks stairs or has to negotiate going in and out of a car. Your little cousin Judah tries to imitate you and clings lovingly to you. You are affectionate with and caring about your pets.

I remember one of your first dogs, Bear, who slept in your room and watched over you. After he died and you were at our house in Port Washington for a Passover Seder, there was a place setting for each family member with place cards made by your sisters. You got a little bowl and put it under the table. You said, "This is for Bear. He is part of our family." Now you have another pet dog, Waffles, and she loves you, too.

You are also helpful, assisting your Dad with household chores and your Mom by cooking and eating very well!

You work so hard at all your undertakings, whether it be school work or in an athletic event. You are a leader, but also a caring teammate who doesn't hog the limelight, (even though you are an outstanding athlete in all sports) but allows each teammate to shine and contribute. You worked to perfect your Hebrew reading and pronunciation for your Bar Mitzvah and gave a fitting and well-formulated *dvar* Torah (interpretation of the Torah part read) about leadership. That day, February 11, 2017, was a joyful celebration for family, friends, coaches, and teammates!

We hope we can enjoy many other celebrations with you and your family. Just keep being Maxwell. We love you.

Grandma Glo and Papa Milosh

Letter to Lexi, my youngest granddaughter:

From the minute you were born, you opened your eyes and seemed to take in the world around you. Though we know infants don't really focus their eyes right away, you seemed, instantly, to be curious about your surroundings. You were so alert!

Your parents were overjoyed that you arrived easily and in good health at a respectable weight of over 7 lbs. It was not only joy, but also gratitude and relief that all went smoothly with mommy's pregnancy and delivery, especially since she had had a dangerous ectopic pregnancy about a year before your birth.

There were visitors to see you including your Nana and Opi, Grandma and Papa; and in the early months, your aunts and uncles and cousins. Auntie J made a special trip to introduce you to your Atlanta cousins. They get excited even now when they know they will see you!

Lexi, you were such a serious little girl. It seemed you were examining everything and trying to figure things out. When you saw someone new, you gave them the once over until you could trust them and relate to them. I was concerned that you smiled so rarely; you were too busy observing.

I really got to know you much better when your Mommy was pregnant with your brother Judah. He was very anxious to be born early and play with you. But mommy had to be on bed rest for about three months so he would be born when he was fully formed and ready to see the sunshine. Fortunately, Nana came in to take care of Mommy so you and daddy could join us in Hilton Head with your cousins Maxwell, Emerson, and Kenzie. We know you both missed mommy in Hilton Head, but we knew she was being well taken care of by Nana 'til you got home. When Nana had to go back to Cape Cod and back to work, I took over and stayed in your house till Judah was born.

It was wonderful that mommy could hug you and read stories to you. But you understood immediately that she had to be in bed and could not go out with you or play with you. You cooperated so beautifully with me. You learned to eat an apple with the peel for snack! We went to the park and to the dock on Eleventh Avenue. We saw big ships. There was a carousel there and a big playground. Remember how we used to race down the hill together? And the fun we had riding on the carousel and having a picnic lunch at one of the tables nearby. One day as I was wheeling you home in the stroller, you said matter of factly, "Grandma, I love you." You were two years old. That melted my heart. We still share that love. When I sing lullabies to you at night and you ask for more songs, that makes the love grow. When you enjoy reading stories with me, that makes the love grow. When you sleep over and give me a tight hug hello and goodbye, that makes the love grow. When you sit with me and have a conversation for fifteen minutes just the two of us before anyone is up—that fills my heart. The more love you give, the more you have to give. We'll never run out of love for each other, Lexi, my little Esther Shoshana bat Mendl Israel.

Thrive, grow, feel, and touch others with your specialness. And go on to enrich the world.

Emerson's and Kenzie's letter (About your birth, February 16, 2006) written September 4, 2016 (updated 2017):

Grandma and Papa were on a vacation to our largest state, Alaska. We knew your mom was pregnant and had a doctor's appointment while we were away. She called us after that appointment and she said, "The doctor told us I'm going to have twins! That changes everything! I hope there is a girl in there somewhere for me." Your brother Maxwell was already about one and a half years old.

Mommy decided to have a caesarian delivery to be safe. She worried that one of you would come out and the second might be stuck. So she made an appointment and was sure that Grandma and Papa would have arrived from New York to take care of Maxwell when she was in the hospital for your birth. We took Maxwell to the hospital to visit the next day. It was a celebration for the entire family. Your mommy got two beautiful little girls. Emerson came out first at 5 lbs., 10 oz. And Kenzie came out next at five pounds. A terrific size for twins.

Grandma made a turkey with roasted potatoes as your Grandpa Charlie and Grandma Linda and Uncle Shawn would be coming over. Before we left, I moved the pan with the turkey covered with aluminum foil on top of the stove all the way to the back. As we entered the hospital room, I heard your daddy talking on the phone to Uncle Shawn, "Bear ate the turkey?" Your dog, Bear, with his terrific sense of smell and his tall body, couldn't resist. He got up on his back legs and he celebrated your birth with a homemade turkey! And we celebrated with Chinese takeout!

Your cribs were head to head, touching each other. At the beginning, you had a nurse who suggested you should be sleeping in the same crib, noses facing each other. That was the sweetest thing to see! It seems that closeness allowed you to form a bond that still exists and will be shared by you both for your entire lives. No matter how many disagreements you will undoubtedly experience, that bond will always unite you with love and support. May you continue to feel this closeness and have someone who will always stand by you.

When you started to make sounds, formulate words, you stood at the head of your cribs, facing each other, you chatted eagerly with sounds and babble. You giggled and bubbled in a language that was truly only your own, but each understanding the other. You kept yourselves occupied this way for long periods of time and needed no other attention from a grown up sometimes for even an hour after you woke up in the morning or after a nap.

Emerson and Kenzie (when older):

I remember a trip from New York to Atlanta with the three of you and daddy. Mommy had to be in New York on business for an extra two days, and Kenzie, you needed surgery on your toe. So I came to be with you and would take a plane home after mommy returned. In the car, I taught you a Yiddish song, "Hot a Yid a Vailbele" ("A Jewish Man Has a Wife"). I sang it in Yiddish, and you joined in and sang the last word in each phrase, i.e. *vailbele, tsoris, kaporis.*

I remember helping your family move to your new home in Buckhead. You had to change schools then. I walked with both of you to your kindergarten and first grade classes when I visited. It was so much fun! It was walking distance from your house and up and down some steep hills. Good exercise for the three of us. You never complained that it was too far or you were tired. I sat in on your class and read a story to the class. Emerson, you composed a song about summer and sang it with your daddy on the guitar. I remember some of your special projects for school, Kenzie. I remember you did one on Egypt and hieroglyphics. I thought that was so advanced for your age and grade.

I remember doing art projects with both of you when you came to visit during Passover and Thanksgiving. We used an open hand with fingers spread wide to create so many wonderful scenes from your imagination. When we visited you in Atlanta, we copied pictures of penguins from the computer, and you made up different stories about them and drew them in various settings.

Today I see you laugh and giggle and sing together. I see you hug each other at camp. I see you disagree and make up. Sometimes even compromise! I love seeing you grow.

We always look forward to our times at Hilton Head where you can play with and take care of your little cousins, Lexi and Judah. They, too, love you so much.

You are "the ladies" as Papa named you when you were very small. And you are becoming very special young ladies now.

Love from Grandma and Papa

Wish for Judah (born October 8, 2013):

May your little eyes behold
the true and the beautiful,
May there be joyous music for your ears to hear
May you experience joyful moments and peals of
laughter,
May your precious heart know
The warmth and wonder of love.
And when you are little no longer,
Judah dear,
May you have the peaceful contentment
Of knowing
That our world is a finer, brighter,
And a lovelier place,
Because you are here.
Grandma Gloria
With love
November 2012

A more current letter to Judah:

Judah, you couldn't wait to get out of your mommy's body to greet the world with your charm, your energy, your generosity, your wit, and your intelligence. Mommy went to the hospital three times to make sure you stayed in and could have enough time to grow into the beautiful boy you are.

And we are all the beneficiaries of your traits. You sometimes get a bit too energetic; not being able to be still for too long, sometimes we think you only know how to run, though you walked by the time you were one year old. It seems your body cannot keep up with your brain.

You keep us all entertained with your witty remarks and poetic definitions. When asked as a three-and-a-half-year-old what falling in love means, you described it: Falling in love is when you go up to the tippy-top of something, and you wiggle around, and you fall, and someone catches you. And everything is all right.

You also know the meaning of very advanced vocabulary words. When daddy told you the name of a musical group called the Rolling Stones you came up with another name for them. You said, "Daddy, they can be called Avalanche!" Some of us don't learn that word 'til eighth or ninth grade. But you knew it by age four!

You could even educate us on the beautiful French language. When at Grandma and Papa's house one day, your sister was complaining about the lunch she got. You stepped right in with your amazing remark: "Don't be a gourmand, be a gourmet."

You are so generous and kind, helping mommy carry groceries even when she only says, "These packages are heavy," you run up and try to grab one of the bags.

You appreciate your sister Lexi's talent in art, giving her a compliment freely. "That's a lovely picture, Lexi."

When I used to leave your apartment 8D in the city before you moved to your new house, I loved it when you ran to the elevator and hugged my knees. And Daddy loves it when you put your head on his shoulder, the picture of contentment. You have so much kindness and love in you.

You helped your daddy find his wallet, indicating that because it was black it was harder to see than a brown wallet, and your home is full of black things. He came back home and found it. You were right! It was on your black banister and blended right in! If it had been brown on a black banister, he would have found it much sooner! You reasoned that logic before you were five years old!

After you lived in your house in Pelham for about four weeks, you expressed a preference for the suburbs over the noise of the city. "It's so peaceful here. I'm meditating. Ohm…"

Judah, may you have that peaceful feeling wherever you are. You are so precious to all of us. Just continue giving us all your wisdom and warmth.

Love you,
Grandma and Papa

Letter to Miles at age eighty-two (August 25, 2016):

Eighty-two! Impressive and gratifying! You have achieved so much;

Your early education, erudition, charm, and sense of humor enabled you to make lasting friendships and impress many people;

You have excelled in your chosen career, which enabled you to support your family with ease and comfort, and you never complained about the hard work or difficult times;

You ran a substantial real estate entity after your mother's death, and the proceeds from it have helped to enrich nine lives.

You have created a family with love, education, travels for your wife, and your two terrific children who make us proud.

You have reached an advanced age when many forget their last names, but you are sharp and can remember details of events and trips that I sometimes question myself whether I was there with you;

Along the road you have and are now handling difficulties that are part of life—disappointments, losses, health issues. Yes, you complain more, but you persevere. You are a mentor and hero to your entire family;

Your five grandchildren love their Papa; and Papa is always renewed and refreshed in their presence.

Miles, enjoy your birthday; enjoy your life! Our blessings beget more blessings: Craig, Lexi, and Judah are coming this weekend, Jordana and crew coming Thanksgiving and Maxwell's Bar Mitzvah is Feb. 11, 2017!

I complain—clean up, throw out, cancel the newspapers, take a walk, we should sell the house—I am stubborn too, knowing I'm in battles I have been waging for years without winning one yet! Love you anyway.

Sergeant Gloria

1. Honoring committee: sitting: Dr. Mordecai Paldiel (1) Morris (Mietek) Friedman; standing: Arnold Friedman, Gloria, Marilyn Starr, Regina Akerman Friedman
2. *Matka* at about age eighty-nine
3. The barn (L-R) Stanka, Matka, Arnold

4. At *Matka's*, Friedmans visit 1978 (L-R) *Matka*, Stanka, Marilyn, Michal; standing: *Matka's* adopted grandson, (name unknown)
5. Michal, *Matka*, Stanka holding a picture of me (1978)
6. *Matka's* legacy on the bimah at the Community synagogue, November 24, 2013
7. Speaking at *Matka's* honoring, November 24, 2013
8. Craig and Jordana emotional when I am presenting *Matka's* certificate to them
9. Craig and Jordana emotional after I present *Matka's* certificate to them
10. My Synagogue involvement: being handed the Torah to dance at Simchat Torah
11. Craig and his wife Katie going to a concert at Lincoln Center
12. Jordana and her husband, Kevin
13. Craig and I at Auschwitz (an MOL trip) 2005
14. Seated: Marek Edelman, Ghetto resistance fighter who stayed in Poland and became a physician. One of his patients was Maria Kowalczyk. As the Friedmans said they got her a Jewish doctor. Ben and Vladka Meed, organizers of the teachers' trip to Poland and Israel in 1993. On the right, Lech Walesa's cabinet member.
15. Publicity for a HMT C event on June 8, 2014. Mine is the bottom hand, on mine is our son Craig's, and on Craig's is his son Judah's hand.

13 14

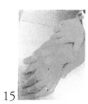

15

CITATIONS PART 5

1. http://kehilalinks.jewishgen.org/Wegrow/cem-ven.html monument in Wegrow
2. https://www.ushmm.org/wlc/en/article.phh?Moduleld=10005685 (UNRRA)
3. Bielawsky, p. 94
4. The Book of Ruth (negation of Ruth's speech to Naomi, Ruth 1:16)

WORKS CITED

Bielawski, Shraga Feivel, Louis W. Liebovich ed. *The Last Jew from Wegrow: The Memoir of a Survivor of the Step-by-Step Genocide in Poland.* Praeger, NY. C. 1991 by Shraga *Feivel Bielawsky & Louis W. Liebovich.*

Friedlander, Saul. (trans. From French by Helen R. Lane). *When Memory Comes.* Other Press. New York. C. 1978 by Editions du Soleil, Paris, France. Translation Copyright 1979 by Farrar, Straus and Giroux, LLC.

Friedlander, Saul. *Where Memory Leads: My Life.* Other Press, NY. C. Saul Friedlander, 2016.

Goldberg, Adara. *Holocaust Survivors in Canada: Exclusion, Inclusion, Transformation.* University of Manitoba Press. C. Adara Goldberg, 2015.

Koblik, Steven. *The Stones Cry Out: Sweden's Response to the Persecution of the Jews 1939-1945.* Holocaust Library, NY. 1988

Kugelmass, Jack and Jonathan Boyarin. Translated & edited by. *From a Ruined Garden: The Memorial Books of Polish Jewry.* Schocken Books, New York. C.1983 by Jack Kugelmass & Jonathan Boyarin.

Meed, Vladka. *On Both Sides of the Wall: Memoirs from the Warsaw Ghetto.* (Moshe Spiegel, translator). Beit Lohamei Haghettaot, Ghetto Fighters House, and Hakibbutz Hameuchad Publishing House. 1977. 1st Published by the Education Committee for the Workmen's Circle, NY. 1948. (This is a translation from: Kehilat Wegrow; Sefer Zikaron; Community of Wegrow; Memorial Book, ed. M.Tamari4Te1Aviv, former residents of Wegrow in Israel, 1961 (citation) #4 Tamari, M. Sefer Zikaron

Tamari, M. ed. Sefer Zikaron. Tel Aviv, Israel, 1961 http://www.jewishgen.org/Yizkor/wegrow/Wegrow.html site of

Weiner, Miriam, (In cooperation with the Polish State Archives. Secaucus, NJ. C. 1997, Miriam Weber.

Wiesel, Elie. All Rivers Run to the Sea -Memoirs. Schocken Books, New York. C. 1995 by Alfred K. Knopf, Inc.

Wiesel, Elie: Marion Wiesel, trans. And the Sea is Never Full. Memoirs 2. Alfred A. Knopf, New York, 1999.

Wingate, Lisa. *Before We Were Yours,* C. 2017, Ballantine Books, New York.

The Holocaust Chronicle: A History in Words and Pictures: C. 2000, Publications International, Ltd; Lincolnwood, III. Louis Weber, CEO. (Not for Profit)

Martyrdom & Resistance, Jan/Feb. 2015, p. 5Wolpe, David. *"Fackenheim's Commandment, 614*th. Jewish Week, 6/9/06,

http://www.virtualmuseum.ca/sgc-cms/expositions-exhibitions/orphelins-orphans/english/themes/where/page2.html war orphans project description

IN GRATITUDE

When such a project is undertaken, it is inevitable that many more people than just the author are involved.

I hereby express my gratitude to those who enabled me to be here today and to live to see this day, *Shechechyanu*. For I would not be here at all if not for certain people who made my survival possible.

The bravery and courage of two women—my mother, Esther Przepiorka, and my *Matka*, Marianna Kowalczyk—allowed me to see this day. Unfortunately, I can never repay that debt of gratitude I owe them.

Gratitude to my Canadian family—Fannie and Abie Morantz, their children, Shirley, Rita, and Stanley, and their sons-in-law—for embracing me, diminishing my trauma, and turning turmoil into tranquility.

To my Aunt Esther and Uncle Max Bernstein for bringing me to these shores, caring for me, and giving me the education to reach my full potential. Subsequently, their three sons—Sam, Phil, and Erwin—and their spouses who embraced me as their little sister and did it so well that their children, for much of their lives, actually believed I was their aunt. Gratitude for helping me with the craft of writing, the idea of writing, and emotional support during writing.

My efforts in this project would have been useless without certain people who came into my life at the right moments for various reasons.

Emily Berkowitz, my editor, cheerleader, and dear friend, whose attention to detail and sincere and valid criticism made me want to continue writing.

Dr. Mordecai Paldiel, who enabled me to honor Maria and Michal Kowalczyk by Yad Vashem and honored me by remaining my mentor, advisor, cheerleader, and friend.

Jennifer Hammer, a family friend and a professional editor, for her invaluable publishing information, prompt responses to my questions, and her helpful edits.

It is their encouragement, knowledge, professionalism, and wise counsel that made this book a reality.

Thank you to my photographer, Robert Kern, (www.robkern.com) for taking my photo under an overhang in NY City, in pouring rain.

My thanks to my publishing assistant, Tina Collins, who has travelled the route to publication with me. She was always available to answer my questions and prompt and clear about providing information and editing status when necessary. At all times she was precise and polite in our communications, whether by e-mail or phone. Thank you, Tina.

The Holocaust Memorial and Tolerance Center for keeping the memory alive, for their professional staff and volunteers who became my teachers and my students.

The Friedman family—Arnold, Regina, Marilyn, and Morris Starr, Morris Friedman—for backing up my testimony for the Righteous Among the Nations award to be given posthumously to the Kowalczyks; their children for their support, and even for their incomplete efforts to honor Marianna Kowalczyk while she was still alive. Those efforts produced the documents from the Jewish Historical Institute, which gave me so much information from her perspective I would never have had. Thus, I was able to get Maria's testimony and her detail about myself and her.

The Jewish Genealogy & Family Heritage Center and The Emanuel Ringelblum Jewish Historical Institute in Warsaw for their meticulous record-keeping and specifically to Anna Przybyszewska Drozd for her sensitivity and her willingness to clarify the documents by translating them for me.

Adara Goldberg for her explanation of the War Orphans Project and for providing my file for the years 1947 to 1957.

Professor Grabowski, for his study of my town, about which I look forward to learning when he publishes it; and for his statistics about the town's survivors, confirming for me how fortunate I was.

Pat Willard of The Gotham Writers Workshop (2008) for helping me to zero in on the arc of the book and my fellow writers in the course for their valuable critique.

My family—my husband, Miles, for his patience as this project has overtaken my life; my children Craig and Jordana, for their ideas, their setting a high bar, and their encouragement; my grandchildren Maxwell, Emerson, Kenzie, Lexi, and Judah, my precious legacy who have, even at a young age, expressed a desire to know our people's history and our family story.

The clergy, the board, the lay leadership, and the congregants of the Community Synagogue for making me proud of my faith and allowing me to grow Jewishly.

May this work serve to preserve the memory of yesterday, a caution (warning) for today, and provide hope for tomorrow.

Gloria Glantz, the 2009 winner of the Spirit of Anne Frank Outstanding Educator Award, is a Holocaust and Tolerance educator, as well as a docent at the Holocaust Memorial and Tolerance Center in Nassau County, New York.

She is a sought-after speaker both nationally and, through videoconferencing, internationally.

She has made it her mission to see that the Shoah is not forgotten. Her dedication to teaching tolerance and acceptance and the lessons of the Holocaust is evidenced in the numerous, highly popular Holocaust and Tolerance courses and workshops she has developed for teachers and students.

In 1993, on a fellowship to study the Holocaust and Resistance, she traveled to Poland and Israel and studied with eminent scholars, including Yehuda Bauer, Martin Gilbert, and Michael Berenbaum.

Gloria resides in Port Washington, New York, with her husband, Miles. They are the proud parents of two children and the grandparents of five.

She can be reached on her website bookiegloriahomes.com

Photo taken by Robert Kern, (www.robkern.@robkerncom).

CPSIA information can be obtained
at www.ICGtesting.com
Printed in the USA
BVHW020229110319
542304BV00024B/529/P

9 781643 007977